Cloud Computing:

A Practical Introduction to the Legal Issues

Cloud Computing:

A Practical Introduction to the Legal Issues

Renzo Marchini

First published in the UK in 2010

by
BSI
389 Chiswick High Road
London W4 4AL

Typeset in Caslon Pro and Franklin Gothic by Monolith – http://www.monolith.uk.com
Printed in Great Britain by Berforts, www.berforts.co.uk

Crown Copyright material is reproduced with the permission of the Controller of HMSO and the Queen's Printer for Scotland. European Union materials (including those of the Article 29 Working Party) are available on http://eur-lex.europa.eu and are copyright © European Union, 1998-2010.

British Library Cataloguing in Publication Data
A catalogue record for this book is available from the British Library

ISBN 978-0-580-70322-5

Contents

To Annette and Max

Acknowledgements

I am indebted foremost to my clients on both the customer and provider side who I have advised over the years in relation to cloud services (sometimes, even before they were even called 'cloud'). Thanks also to the many IT law and information security professionals with whom I have enjoyed discussing the issues covered in this book, including Amer Moorhead and his team at Ariba and John Moss at Salesforce.com, all of whom are involved daily in cloud law. Special mention should go to Andreas Fuchsberger of Microsoft, Christine Giraudon of Salesforce.com and Mark Watts of Bristows for their helpful comments on the manuscript, and likewise also to Dick Price of Beacon IT with particular thanks for his very expert comments on the ISO/IEC 27000 series section. Any errors are of course my own.

I would also like to thank my colleagues at Dechert (in particular, Paul Kavanagh and Kate Tebbutt) for support and encouragement. I also received useful help from the excellent trainee solicitors that passed through my supervision while the manuscript was being developed (Ailsa Fudge, Iria Giuffrida and David Lawne).

Thanks, above all, to my wife and son, Annette and Max, for their love and support and for their understanding as to the time commitment involved in writing this book; and especially to Max for choosing the cover.

Lastly, my thanks go to all at BSI especially to my editor, Julia Helmsley, for her experienced guidance to a first-time author, to David Fatscher for his initial suggestion that we collaborate on this book and to Siobhán FitzGerald for steering it through production.

1 Foreword

1.1 Introduction

There is no universally accepted definition of 'cloud computing' and the term means various things in different contexts and indeed to different people. It is a paradigm shift in how computer resources are acquired. Some doubt that there is anything new about the cloud, pointing out the fact that many of the features which are said to be part of this paradigm have in fact existed for quite some time in other (non-cloud) technologies and services.

A fuller definition of the terminology necessary to serve the aim of this book is set out further on. However, in summary, cloud computing refers to the delivery of computing capability (whether of an application software variety, an infrastructure delivery, or otherwise) by a provider remotely over a communications link, allowing for no actual installation (of the software or the infrastructure) at the customer site.

It is not only enterprises that are using cloud services. The history of the consumer cloud is intimately linked to the history of the internet. Many common and well established web services such as email services (e.g. Hotmail) and photo sharing services (e.g. Flickr) have existed since the early days of the web, but over the last few years the willingness of consumers to trust often quite sensitive personal information to social networking sites (Facebook, LinkedIn and others, all of which are 'cloudy' in nature) has taken the trust to a new level.

This book attempts to identify, discuss and elucidate many of the common legal issues that arise from this paradigm shift. It is intended to be practical and assumes very little by way of legal knowledge. In respect of the more difficult legal issues (such as perhaps data protection and security), a practical understanding necessarily depends on a fuller exposition of the underlying law – which is provided – but again it is hoped that the end result is nonetheless useful to those not legally qualified.

One of the problems with analysing cloud issues from a legal perspective is the multinational aspect: the fact that many countries may be involved in a particular cloud provision. A customer in country A, for example, may use a SaaS (software as a service) offered by a provider in country B, who in turn acquires infrastructure capacity in countries C, D and/or E (depending on the current price in each). Whilst this book is based on English law, many of the issues which arise (in particular in relation to risk allocation and service provisions in contracts) will be common across different legal systems. The issues surrounding data protection discussed in chapters 5 to 7 are very similar throughout Europe as a result of a common adoption of the same Data Protection Directive [1]. Issues such as service description (chapter 10) and service levels (chapter 11) are matters of technical capability, business assessment, negotiation and risk, and are largely independent of the law of the country in which either the customer or the provider reside. As such, non-UK readers may also find it interesting.

Whilst this book is intended as a practical guide to these issues, it goes without saying that it is no substitute for considered legal advice.

1.2   History and development

For present purposes, the history of computing could perhaps be summarized as follows:

a) 1940s: early beginnings in isolated research centres;

b) 1960s to 1970s: mainframe computers and dumb terminals; bureau processing;

c) 1980s: the rise of the PC and Microsoft; standardization of hardware; the rise of independent software vendors; commencement of large scale outsourcing;

d) 1990s: the advent of networking and the internet; .com boom; application service provision;

e) 2000s: .com bust; the distribution of ever-increasing accessibility through broadband and Wi-Fi; the rise of Google and the consumer cloud;

f) 2010s: virtualization; green-computing; the rise of the business cloud (perhaps).

As this very approximate time line is examined, it is possible to detect a number of characteristics relevant to why the cloud is happening now. First, it is notable that in the early days of computing, hardware manufacturers were the dominant players, and software languages were tailored for specific machines. Computing power was concentrated in the few and the idea of processing data through a remote service (a bureau service) was not controversial (as it is now), simply often a necessity. As time progressed, it was possible for entities to handle internally their own IT requirements and the in-house IT department was born. Time moved on again and it was recognized that that is not often very efficient. Computing could be left to the experts and outsourcing (in many guises) began. Cloud computing can be seen as just one type of outsourcing, and indeed there are some who consider there to be little difference between what is now labelled 'cloud' and what went before and that there is simply a hype surrounding it.

Larry Ellison, the CEO and founder of Oracle, for one, has been very critical of the surrounding hype. He has given a number of widely quoted interviews, including one in 2008 in which he made the point that the definition is so wide that it includes everything that Oracle actually does, comparing it disparagingly to women's fashion and referring to it as 'complete gibberish'.[1]

In the same interview, he also makes the point that all these predictions about how things would change are so often wrong. The PC would kill mainframes; they did not. Open source software would kill software houses; it has not.

Others, implicitly recognizing that there is something new happening, are critical of the movement. Richard Stallman, the founder of the GNU project and open source software pioneer, has called cloud computing 'stupidity' – a means for the gullible to be locked into particular providers (once those providers have the user's data in a proprietary format). The issue of provider lock-in is explored in chapter 9.

Whether or not there is a real paradigm shift might depend on the type of cloud service that is being talked about. As the brief timeline shows in this clause, the idea of obtaining use of a software application remotely is as old as computing; early software use involved access to mainframes with distributed dumb terminals or to data processing power through bureau services. So, in a sense, at least one of the types of cloud services (SaaS) might be nothing particularly new from what has gone before but with one important distinction – the distinction of scale. It has simply become more prevalent. As such there is at least a germ of truth in what Larry Ellison says: much of it has been done before. Other types of cloud offering, for example, the idea of acquiring server capacity in a 'utility-like' manner (IaaS – infrastructure as a service), paid for as you go and scaled as you need, may well represent a fundamental shift in the acquisition of technology motivated by many concerns: cost pressures, economies of scale, energy efficiency.

More pertinent perhaps is the issue not so much of whether this is hype but rather – even if it is hype – why it is happening now. Arguably, it is happening now because it is a real phenomenon driven by a desire to minimize computing costs, have flexibility and be more efficient – a desire matched by IT providers tailoring their offerings on the back of easily accessible high-speed connectivity through the internet and otherwise.

It seems likely that, new or not, the cloud is here to stay.

---

[1] Larry Ellison, Oracle OpenWorld, 25 September 2008.

1.3 What is cloud computing?

There are many different views on the question, including much academic, technical and business disagreement as to what the salient features are. For present purposes, broadly, cloud computing refers to the delivery of computing capability by a provider remotely over a communications link. It comes in many different varieties, serving a wide variety of computing needs, and there are inevitably arguments and discussion over what are the essential elements of a cloud offering. The following are the most important features which trigger the application of legal issues dealt with in this book. A typical cloud offering will involve (some if not all of) the following features:

a) there will be no actual requirement for software installation at the customer site (except for a standard internet browser);

b) the customer will be using software operated by the provider on servers controlled by the provider (or on behalf of the provider);

c) the customer can pay on a usage basis;

d) the delegation to the provider of responsibility for keeping software up to date;

e) the delegation to the provider of responsibility for keeping data secure; and

f) the delegation to the provider of responsibility for managing the hardware.

This list is not set in stone and not all of these features are essential; many offerings that are properly called cloud may omit one or more. Some would argue that the list is in fact too short and, for example, that an important feature of a genuine cloud offering is that there is in fact no clearly allocated server for a particular customer and/or that different customers are serviced using the same 'instance' of the software in a multi-tenancy model. Where a particular feature's presence or absence is important to a particular issue which is covered in this book that will be made clear.

A basic categorization is between on the one hand a cloud service that provides use of software remotely and on the other hand a cloud service that provides use of hardware or other infrastructure components. The next sections explain expressions that are frequently used to describe some of the different aspects of cloud. Some identify the type of service, others the deployment models of the service, and lastly some identify different technologies involved.

1.4 Cloud service types

A number of terms are frequently used to describe the cloud service types as follows.

1.4.1 SaaS – software as a service

The quintessential cloud offering: application software is no longer downloaded or installed onto the user's computer (server or PC) but instead is provided remotely by the provider, perhaps through a web interface. It is subscribed to, not licensed.

There are a myriad of examples, perhaps the most-quoted one being Salesforce.com's Customer Relationship Management (CRM) service.

1.4.2 IaaS – infrastructure as a service

The idea here is that the hardware (or other infrastructure) needs of an organization are met remotely by the provider. The provider takes responsibility for the customer's processing needs, normally of servers but perhaps also of storage devices. Web hosting services (where a company's websites would be hosted by a specialist company) have always been, in a sense, a very simple type of IaaS – a server being provided for the specific need of giving the customer a web presence. However, that concept has now evolved so that the servers on which the site is hosted will be 'virtual' and 'scalable'. In this regard, a term that is often seen is 'cloud hosting', a type of IaaS, providing the benefits of scalable, on demand, and – say the providers – low-cost web hosting to many companies.

IaaS is wider than simply web hosting. The widest variety of hardware and for the widest range of uses is available. Amazon's cloud offerings are prominent examples: Amazon's Simple Storage Service (Amazon S3) provides a cloud storage service whilst its Elastic Compute Cloud (Amazon EC2) provides server capacity.

1.4.3 PaaS – platform as a service

This is IaaS with added value designed to allow smaller providers quickly and cheaply to set up SaaS services. A potential provider of a SaaS service will of course still need infrastructure upon which it can operate its software for its customers. It could take a two step approach: first, develop its own software in a traditional manner and then, secondly, deploy it on an IaaS offering acquired from elsewhere. A PaaS solution brings these two steps together. An additional layer (the 'platform') of software is provided over and above the infrastructure that appears in IaaS. This platform allows the customer to develop its own software application (with the provider's development tools) and deploy that software application through the infrastructure. Whilst clearly of immense use to smaller businesses keen to set up a cloud business with minimal effort and investment in more traditional development tools, an overriding issue for many in using this type of offering is the fact that the application thus developed will then only be capable of running on that particular cloud platform. There is therefore a particular and pronounced issue of vendor lock-in. Prominent examples are Google App Engine and Microsoft Azure.

1.4.4 Utility computing

The idea behind utility computing is that computing technology can be switched on and off in much the same way as electricity and other utilities. For the purpose of this book, the term adds little to what is included within the term 'IaaS'.

1.4.5 Grid computing or distributed computing

This is a type of computing network where the capacity of a large number of computers accessed through a network is available to particular types of users. University and scientific computing capacity is often structured in this manner so that heavy processing tasks (e.g. meteorology) can make efficient use of vast computing resources when they might otherwise be idle. Another example of this, which has captured the popular imagination, is the Search for Extraterrestrial Intelligence (SETI@home) project, where a great quantity of data from radio telescopes gathered by astronomers is sent out to numerous home computers. The software on the home computers runs when the screen saver is on (or is otherwise idle) to try and detect patterns in the data which might indicate extraterrestrial life.

1.4.6 Other cloud service types

The computing industry seems to know no bounds in creating new 'aaS' terms, and the following are all beginning to appear in literature: business (or Business Process) as a service (BaaS), storage as a service (StaaS), desktop as a service (DaaS) and so on.

1.4.7 A stack of services

Figure 1 illustrates how different types of providers can in fact 'sit on top of each other'. An understanding of the existence of this stack is important as it determines, for example, where in fact the customer's data might be. The customer will ordinarily only contract with one party; when it is acquiring a SaaS service, it will only contract with the person at the top of the diagram. The data might however be in the actual possession of the IaaS provider (and, to complicate matters, there could be a subcontractor below that provider).

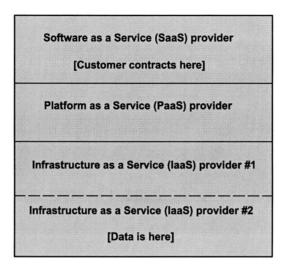

Figure 1. Different types of offerings built on top of each other

1.5 Deployment models

There are terms that define the type of person to whom a particular service is deployed (whether SaaS, PaaS or IaaS):

1.5.1 Public cloud

Most cloud services are used by anyone willing to acquire them, and this is what is meant by a 'public cloud' offering.

1.5.2 Private cloud (sometimes called an 'internal cloud')

Some aspects of cloud computing can be adopted without involving an external provider. A private cloud is when cloud-like services are deployed within a large group, say, by a dedicated service company providing software or infrastructure services remotely that is useable by any of the members of that group. Some commentators would add a requirement that there must also be dynamic availability (depending on demand) of applications or resources before the offering is truly a private cloud. For some organizations, a private cloud may initially be a stepping stone on a transition path to use of a full cloud offering.

1.5.3 Community cloud

A cloud service used by a specific group of persons (the members of a particular community).

1.5.4   Hybrid cloud

When an organization uses more than one type of cloud (or more than one offering from different cloud providers), they are using a hybrid.

1.5.5   Consumer cloud

Many of the services used by consumers on the internet are cloud services. Social networking sites involve the consumer storing their (sometimes very) personal data on services under the control of Facebook, Bebo, LinkedIn and the like. Likewise, email services such as Hotmail and Gmail are true cloud services. Of course, consumers do not use those expressions and do not generally consider such issues as data security and server location.

1.6   Technological terminology

The cloud model brings with it a number of technical terms (describing particular technologies which may feature in different services or deployments) which will need to be understood by those navigating the legal issues.

1.6.1   Virtualization

This term normally describes a technology under which software that an enterprise needs runs not on a specific server, but on a 'virtual' server. Many IaaS services depend on this technology (but they are not synonymous). The virtual server might be spread across a number of different physical servers, and the IT infrastructure manages the load (dynamically and invisibly to the applications themselves and certainly the users) to ensure that the most efficient use of the underlying physical computing power is made. The term can also cover the reverse situation where a number of different virtual servers operate on one physical server. Whilst common in IaaS offerings, a virtualized infrastructure can also be implemented by the enterprise's own IT department (perhaps as part of a private cloud).

Virtualization software exists for home consumers' use also, allowing the host desktop to appear as a number of different virtual PCs.

1.6.2   Multi-tenancy

This is a term that describes how a particular 'instance' of software running on a server (or servers) is used by the cloud provider to provide services to many of its customers. It is an important concept as it appears time and time again in contract negotiations in relation to cloud offerings; in particular, it will often be used by service providers to justify many of the stances they take in their contract terms.

The basic idea is that the same copy of the software is running data for many customers at the same time.

Given the importance of the concept, a further word of explanation might be helpful for the non-technically minded. In a traditional deployment of software, when software is run on a computer internal to an organization (this is a simplification), one copy of the software is brought into the memory of the computer (from the hard drive) and that copy accesses and processes that organization's data. That is one 'instance' of the software in memory. Another customer using the same software may well be using the identical software (in the sense of same version number) but it will be a different instance (not least because it is on a different computer).

Now assume that the software is provided remotely by a SaaS provider. The provider might run the same program a number of different times (multiple instances) concurrently on the same server; each instance would process different data for different clients. However, it would also be possible for the provider to run just one instance to simultaneously process two different sets of data (for two different clients). Each set of data in this scenario is a 'tenant' in the instance, hence 'multi-tenancy'. Naturally, as the two sets of data might belong to separate clients, security and a proper segregation of data within the one instance is paramount.

1.7 Comparisons with other types of IT services

Cloud computing may well be new, but various aspects of this model do feature in other more traditional types of IT offerings – from the recent past (out of which cloud may have in part evolved) but even from the more distant past. As such, many of the legal issues that arise in cloud will be familiar from these other scenarios. With that in mind, and with a view of applying legal principles which had been applied to these other types of IT offerings, it will be useful to identify similarities and differences between cloud computing and those offerings with which cloud shares features.

1.7.1 Outsourcing

Outsourcing involves the handing over of an IT function previously provided internally to an external provider. It might involve the outsourcing of the whole IT department (data centres, all support staff, in-house development teams, and so on) but might be more limited. It can be similar both to IaaS (as the provider will manage the infrastructure) and to SaaS (as software functionality may be served to the customer remotely). The provider will of course have to handle security. It might also (depending on what is outsourced) involve the creation of applications and the delivery of software to users and so be similar to PaaS.

1.7.2 Managed services

This is a type of outsourcing where servers and software are managed remotely from the customer by the service provider. Similar in some instances to an IaaS service, the provider will provide remote access to the service, manage the infrastructure, and have actual possession of data. It does not necessarily involve (but can have) virtualization. When there is virtualization, it can have usage charging models. The location of the data centre is usually known.

1.7.3 Batch computing/service bureau

An example from the earlier days of computing, this is the provision of remote data processing by dedicated software on servers. Customer data is input, processing is carried out, and data returned to the customer (or action undertaken). Similar in some instances to a SaaS service, data is held by the provider and the provider keeps software up to date. Again, the location of the data centre is usually known.

1.7.4 ASP – application service provision

A term (from the late 1990s and early 2000s) that has somewhat fallen out of fashion, but in essence is simply SaaS. An application is provided as a service remotely.

1.7.5 Client/Server

A software architecture that divides processing between a client (or clients), which requests the service, and a server, which fulfils them. It is similar (and an early precursor) to SaaS, at least when the architecture is used externally. When used internally, it is similar to SaaS on a private cloud. Normally, the server and client side are managed by the same person and that is perhaps a distinction to be drawn.

1.7.6 Conclusion on differences

As can be seen, therefore, many cloud features existed in pre-cloud days (so maybe Mr Ellison is right). The one feature that is definitely new is that which – as we will see – presents the greatest difficulty: the customer does not necessarily know where the data is. Other parts of the paradigm are familiar with, and the legal issues that arise are similar to, what has gone before. Data is held by a provider who takes care of security, service level commitments are necessary, and so on.

1.8 Why now?

Whilst it is probably true that SaaS has been around for a while, there are a number of reasons as to why the concept of cloud computing has attracted such traction recently. First, the size of the players involved means that anything they do will have serious and widespread repercussions. Amazon (and its like) has built such large data centres, literally the size of many football pitches, to fulfil its requirements. Naturally its requirements for IT resources vary over time with peak demand, in particular, around Christmas (in common with many retailers). But it is not just around the holidays; demand varies throughout the day and over the week. Amazon identified that it had to do something with its spare capacity and began in 2006 to offer that capacity to other businesses through its Amazon EC2 service, allowing them to acquire infrastructure on a pay as you go model. Where Amazon led, many other IT giants (Google and Microsoft) followed.

A second reason as to why there is at present such an acceleration into the cloud is the recognition by many users of technology of the wastage in their own server capacities, and thus a drive towards the saving of costs. Linked to the cost saving is the current green agenda and a move towards 'green computing'. This latter term aims to identify an imperative to be more eco-friendly in sourcing computing power. It has been estimated that a typical business is wasting at least 75% of the capacity it has for storage and 85% of the capacity it has for processing power. Sharing resources is a way of more efficiently using computing technology.

Thirdly, the Amazon model allows very large economy of scale and that too has had a major impact when IT budgets increasingly take a bigger share of a company's cost base.

Lastly, it is quite simply becoming technically possible. Broadband is widespread and now reliable, leased lines are prevalent, and it is ever easier for businesses to make the leap and trust the remote provision of services.

1.9   Overview of this book

This book is intended to be a practical introduction on legal issues in cloud computing suitable for those either providing such services or considering an acquisition. It is designed to be read as a practical introduction and the hope is that it will be of interest to lawyers and non-lawyers alike, anyone navigating the difficult legal issues which might arise. Where the legal issues arising depend on some background knowledge, not much is assumed. Instead, a short introduction is provided so as to make this as self-contained as possible.

In any cloud situation, in order to navigate the various legal issues that arise, it is important first to identify the relevant body of law that applies. We address this issue in chapter 2.

The next series of chapters deal with information security (chapter 3) and then data protection in chapters 4 (basics), 5 (putting personal data into the cloud), 6 (moving personal data outside of Europe) and 7 (data breach notification).

We then move onto issues that arise as a result of contracts. Chapter 8 deals with software licensing issues (including issues around moving legacy systems onto cloud infrastructures and open source). In chapter 9 we deal with a number of issues relating to customer data. Sometimes providers want to use data for their own purposes; this can be controversial and is explored here. It also covers the critical issue of customer lock-in and access to data. Chapter 10 covers issues relating to definition of the service and the ability of the provider to change the service, whilst chapter 11 deals with service levels and service credits. A provider's ability to limit its potential liability by contractual language is dealt with in chapter 12. In chapter 13 we move to issues that arise in specific sectors (financial services, the public sector and consumers). Finally, in chapter 14 we look to the future of cloud law.

1.10   Contracting for the cloud

One further point should be noted at this stage. Throughout this book we discuss how a contract might deal with a particular issue to address a concern of the customer and how the customer might want to critically review language suggested by the provider. Implicit in this discussion is the idea that the provider will entertain a request that the contract be negotiated. It is worthwhile exploring therefore the extent to which contracts are being negotiated.

One aspect of cloud computing which is often cited as being different from other outsourcing deals is the take-it-or-leave-it aspect of the provision. In keeping with the commercial and technical advantages of the solution being easy to set up, easy to scale, and easy to control charges, it is also equally easy to contract: a customer simply accepts the provider's terms without question. This is very true in relation to many provisions available at relatively low cost and possibly without any interaction except through the provider's website. It is not however true of substantial acquisitions by enterprises. Contracts are still individually negotiated. Many cloud providers may present their contracts as standard and not invite negotiation. Nonetheless, customers can request changes to the 'standard'. Whether the provider agrees to those requests will depend on the negotiating power of the customer. Consumers and most small businesses, each acquiring a very standard cloud offering, will have no scope for negotiating terms. That is not the case for substantial enterprises negotiating as equals with a cloud provider. The bigger the potential contract, the greater the scope for the cloud provider moving from its standard position to secure the deal.

2 Which law of the cloud?

2.1 Introduction

Laws differ from country to country. The nature of the cloud is that it is extremely likely that more than one country is involved in a particular cloud deployment (unless a customer can be confident that its provider and the data centre are all in the same country). Therefore, whenever the legality of any activity is questioned, or consideration is given as to how to roll-out or acquire a compliant service, it is important first to identify the relevant law that applies. Then an assessment can be made as to what that law says. More than one law may apply. For example, to answer the question 'what are the legal requirements around security?', you first need to identify the legal system to apply. In the cloud, not only may activities take place across a number of borders, but it may not even be possible to identify in which country some aspects of the activity take place. So, for example, if the customer is in the UK, but the provider is in California, is security assessed under UK standards or Californian[2] standards?

In a typical cloud scenario (to the extent there is such a thing) there are at least four legal systems contending for consideration. The law to look at might be the legal system of the country where the customer is, where the provider is, where the data is stored, and that of the individual to whom the data refers.

In any field (not just cloud) such questions are often resolved by reference to one of a number of international treaties often passed at the European level (but some have wider reach or are bilateral). Two prominent examples are the European instruments known as 'Rome I' [2], dealing with the law that is to apply to a contract, and 'Rome II' [3], dealing with the law to apply to non-contractual obligations ('torts', such as negligence). These instruments are general in the sense that they apply to all types of activities. In relation to any complex issue involving a 'choice of law', a two-stage approach is needed. First, these and other such instruments will need to be consulted to determine which country's laws are involved. Only then can that country's laws be applied to the activity or issue. It goes without saying that the laws are not created

---

[2]   The US have different legal systems in each of their 50 states.

specifically with cloud services in mind and therefore given the character of the cloud it is not always possible to give definitive answers to the issues that may arise. A discussion of these issues (even as they apply to the cloud) quickly gets very technical and as such is beyond the scope of the book. But a brief description may be helpful.

We begin however with some examples that show how these issues are not theoretical. Disputes as to applicable law have already arisen.

2.2 International disputes as to applicable (cloud) law

Although there are few real incidents of such 'conflicts of law' in the business cloud area, there have already been a few prominent cases in the consumer cloud field. Amongst the stories that made the news in the last few years are Yahoo! in Belgium and Google in Brazil, which are both examples of US cloud providers being compelled to give up data (which was outside that country) by the courts of a country into which they are selling services.

2.2.1 Yahoo! in Belgium

Belgian fraud investigators were investigating people who used the Yahoo! mail service (a consumer cloud offering) in order to engage in an online crime. The service was sold from the US into Belgium. The investigators asked Yahoo! to help identify the criminals by giving up whatever data it had relating to their registration on the service in order to assist in identification. Yahoo! refused. It argued that as it was a Californian company the investigators should proceed through a formal treaty and seek the assistance of the US authorities (who definitely had jurisdiction over Yahoo!). Yahoo! had no actual presence in Belgium and did not actively market in Belgium. Its service is open to people in any country of the world and it has no means of verifying in what country the user actually resides. The Belgian law enforcement agencies responded that Yahoo! was also a Belgian company as its services are available in Belgium. Whilst in March 2009 Yahoo! was fined for failing to hand over the details, this was overturned on appeal in June 2010. It was widely reported in the press that the Belgian Court of Appeal in Ghent broadly agreed with Yahoo!'s arguments.[3]

2.2.2 Google in Brazil

In August 2006, a Brazilian court ordered Google to release information on its social networking site (Orkut), and stated that they would face a $23,000 a day fine until such data was released. The information was said to be useful to find criminals who had been using the service for criminal activities (child pornography

---

[3] The judgement is only available in Flemish.

and selling drugs). Similarly to the Yahoo! case just mentioned, Google argued that it could not do so on the grounds that the requested information was in the US and was therefore not subject to Brazilian laws. There was negotiation despite this argument and eventually Google provided the Brazilian police with access to data by means of a special administration tool for deleting or blocking illegal content.

In July 2008, it was widely reported in the press that the Brazilian authorities and Google reached an agreement to try and prevent illegal material on Orkut. The agreement, which may well have been the first of its kind internationally, stated that Google would employ filtering technology to block and remove illegal content on Orkut; it would also provide evidence in suspected crimes against minors when presented with a Brazilian judicial order without requiring international legal manoeuvring.

2.3 Which law applies to the cloud?

2.3.1 Introduction

The determination of which country's law applies to a particular cloud situation depends on the type of issue about which there is concern. For each legal topic (data protection, contract, liability issues, criminal law, and so on), the answer may – unfortunately – be different. This chapter considers the main areas of law that need to be considered and gives an outline of how an English court would answer the question.

2.3.2 Data protection

The European Data Protection Directive [1] contains its own separate rules for deciding which country's data protection rules apply. This is examined in detail in 4.5, but for now it is worth noting that the rules look not at the residency or nationality of the individuals concerned, but rather at where the person 'controlling' the data (who is likely to be the cloud customer) is based.

2.3.3 Contract law

The rights and obligations of parties to a contract (including such rules as to whether a contract is formed, whether provisions limiting liability are 'reasonable', how they can be terminated) need to be judged against a body of contract law. These laws differ, sometimes remarkably, from country to country. The UK is subject to rules on the choice of law in contracts which are set out in a European Union regulation commonly known as Rome I [2]. This states broadly that subject to certain exceptions, a court should apply the law chosen by the parties. Of course, well-drafted contracts will always be explicit about the law the parties agree should govern their relationship. When a cloud contract involves entities in more than one country there is an obvious choice to be made between the law of the country where the provider is based and that where the customer is located. It is possible indeed for the contract to choose that the law under which it is to be interpreted is that of a completely unrelated country, and some US cloud providers will choose, say, English law to apply to all their European contracts. If there was no choice by the parties, Rome I sets out a set of rules for common situations including the following, which is likely to be applicable to a cloud situation: 'a contract for the provision of services shall be governed by the law of the country where the service provider has his habitual residence'. A cloud provider is therefore likely to be able to argue that its 'home' law applies.

A cloud provider cannot however be absolutely certain that its choice of law will prevail as there are exceptions to the general rules. In particular, consumers are protected. A choice of law must not deprive the consumer of protection afforded to him by provisions that cannot be excluded by agreement, for example, the Unfair Contract Terms Act 1977 [4] (see 12.5). In addition, and not only for consumers, the parties cannot agree to remove the operation of certain 'mandatory' provisions relevant in a particular country. These are defined as provisions which are regarded as crucial by a country for safeguarding its public interests, to such an extent that they are applicable to any situation falling within their scope, irrespective of the law chosen by the parties. Lastly, the application of the law chosen by the parties may be refused if such application is manifestly incompatible with the public policy in a particular country.

2.3.4 Liability issues

Liability to persons with whom there is no contractual relationship is mostly covered by a body of laws called 'tort'. Tort issues might arise when the cloud service is accessible by members of the public (such as consumer cloud services). There might be libels committed, negligent advice, infringement of confidential information, and so on. Torts can cross borders (the innocent party can be in a different country from the perpetrator) and in attempting to answer what law is to apply in such a situation, the UK courts will look to another European instrument: Rome II [3]. This states that, subject to a number of exceptions (which are outside the scope of this brief introduction), the applicable law to non-contractual obligations is the law of the country in which the damage occurs irrespective of where the events giving rise to the damage occurred or where the indirect consequences of that event occur. However, where the person claimed to be liable and the person suffering damage both have their habitual residence in the same country at the time the damage occurs, the law of that country will apply.

2.3.5   Ecommerce Directive's 'Country of Origin' rule

The European Ecommerce Directive of 2000 [5] is intended to ensure that European businesses operating online do not have to worry that their online activities comply with legal requirements throughout the 27 different countries that are members of the European Union but instead only have to ensure that their activities are lawful in the 'country of origin'. The scope of the legislation covers such things as laws relating to requirements to get licences from particular regulators, sales promotion and advertising laws, and so on. In other words, issues which enforcement authorities (rather than, say, contracting partners) might take an interest in. It does not cover issues relating to data protection or to contracts which might be entered into online or other 'private law' issues (all of which are dealt with by the areas of law just mentioned). Unfortunately, the legislation is far from easy to decipher and there remains much controversy throughout Europe as to the exact scope of the rules.

This will be more of interest to cloud providers with a web presence open to the public. In relation to non-contractual activities, they should – in theory – only have to worry about regulation and law in their home jurisdiction; more accurately, in the country in which they are established. They need not worry about other European laws. (However, the Directive says nothing about the laws of other non-European Union countries to which the provider might be selling services.)

To decide on where a provider is 'established' the focus is on where 'an economic activity' is being undertaken on an ongoing basis. It is clear that the location of the servers is not determinative of the issue (although it may be a relevant factor). A cloud provider with offices and staff in the UK providing a service based upon a foreign IaaS or PaaS offering would be considered to be established in the UK (and not where the IaaS/PaaS has its data centre).

PRACTICAL TIP

Even if a cloud provider supplying services to the public complies with all laws in the country in which it is 'established', it may still have to consider the laws of other countries in the EU as some countries (e.g. France) interpret the Ecommerce Directive differently. Whilst checking all countries is impractical, a provider might focus on those countries where there might be a risk of real enforcement action.

2.4   Law enforcement agencies' ability to obtain data

2.4.1   Introduction

Most countries have wide-ranging powers for law enforcement agencies to obtain intelligence for criminal investigatory and anti-terrorist purposes. Nonetheless, it is the US power to do so that particularly causes controversy and is often mentioned in cloud commentary: the US Patriot Act [6].[4] In essence, this allows US law enforcement to demand that holders of information provide relevant agencies with that information. It was passed in the wake of the terrorist atrocities of 11 September 2001.

Before exploring a little further, it is as well to remember that all countries have laws allowing their law enforcement agencies to obtain data. The UK certainly does. There are wide powers to obtain data for national security reasons and the prevention and detection of crime. We mention three examples. The Regulation of Investigatory Powers Act 2000 [7] allows the Secretary of State to issue a warrant authorizing or requiring the person to whom it is addressed to intercept communications in the course of their transmission. The Intelligence Services Act 1994 [8] allows the Secretary of State to issue a warrant authorizing the otherwise unlawful entry into, or interference with, someone's property – for example, for the purpose of eavesdropping or conducting a secret intelligence search. Lastly, the Police Act 1997 [9] contains similar provisions to the Intelligence Services Act 1994 and provides for the authorization of interference with property and wireless telegraphy in the course of intrusive surveillance operations conducted by, for example, the police, the Office of Fair Trading and HM Revenue & Customs within the UK.

2.4.2   The US Patriot Act

Nonetheless, for reasons which might be more to do with a greater distrust of foreign laws (compared to the laws of one's own country) than any substantial difference in the scope of the powers that the authorities have, it is the US Patriot Act [6] which attracts most attention in cloud discussions and so it is that which is explored a little further. The US Patriot Act is a piece of anti-terrorism legislation that was a response to the events of 11 September 2001. Among other things, it expands the intelligence gathering and surveillance powers of US law enforcement agencies.

The Patriot Act [6] allows US authorities to obtain records (i.e. data) to protect against international terrorism. Foreign intelligence gathering need only be a 'significant' purpose, rather than the only purpose, of the searches or surveillance in the US. The Act also expanded the circumstances under which the FBI can

---

[4]   The full name of the legislation is **U**niting and **S**trengthening **A**merica by **P**roviding **A**ppropriate **T**ools **R**equired to **I**ntercept and **O**bstruct **T**errorism (hence, 'US Patriot' Act).

compel financial institutions, phone companies and Internet Service Providers (ISPs) secretly to disclose information about their customers. The FBI is required only to establish that the information it seeks is relevant to an authorized intelligence investigation. Thus, although enacted primarily for anti-terrorism purposes, its provisions allow use for, and have in fact been used in, ordinary criminal investigations that have no terrorism feature. It is not only European data protection regulators that have a distrust for such wide-ranging powers; the US Patriot Act has certainly caused problems for authorities outsourcing in Canada.

The laws of two Canadian provinces (those of British Columbia and Nova Scotia) contain restrictions on public bodies transferring personal information outside of Canada, including to the United States. In 2004, the British Columbian government (as part of its privatization of aspects of health provision) announced that it was contracting with two US companies. There was an immediate public outcry in relation to the possibility that sensitive private medical information could find its way – through the Patriot Act – into the hands of US law enforcement agencies (even when the data never in fact left Canada). The British Columbia Government and Service Employees' Union (BCGSU) commenced legal action to prevent this outsourcing. They argued that the possibility of access by the US authorities would contravene the province's data protection legislation (the Freedom of Information and Protection of Privacy Act (FOIPPA) [10]). (As it happens, the court disagreed and found that there was sufficient privacy.) The local law was in the end changed, prohibiting any access to data except from within Canada.

2.4.3   Application to the cloud

The US Patriot Act [6] would allow the US authorities to obtain data belonging to a UK cloud customer residing in a server farm of a US cloud provider. In the following chapters we describe how data protection law (and in particular the restrictions on transferring data abroad) impact upon cloud. In brief, a cloud customer sending data to the US should undertake due diligence and take into account the legal regime in the US and therefore the potential impact of the Patriot Act. The UK data protection regulator, the Information Commissioner's Office (ICO), has specifically referred to a customer taking the Patriot Act into account in the necessary risk assessment as part of a possible outsourcing to the US.[5] Needless to say, this does not mean of course that a provider in the US should never be used. In many and perhaps most circumstances, there will be no real problem. Greater care will be needed perhaps when the data is particularly sensitive. When outsourcing goes ahead, the ICO points out UK customers should

---

[5] See for example both (i) The eighth data protection principle and international data transfers, Version 3.0, 17.12.08 and (ii) Data Protection Good Practice Note Outsourcing – a guide for small and medium sized businesses, version 2.1, 09.04.09.

make sure they have procedures and measures in place to deal with any requests for information that may be received under the US Patriot Act. Such measures might include a requirement to refer US authorities' requests to the customer. The ICO is considering a traditional outsourcing contract, rather than cloud, but the point is equally applicable. Indeed, it applies not only to the US Patriot Act but also to the legislation in any country in which the cloud provider may be located.

> **PRACTICAL TIP**
>
> Cloud customers should consider including obligations in a contract that require the provider to refer (where legally able to do so) to the customer any requests for data from external agencies.
>
> If a cloud provider accommodates such a suggestion in the contract, it will need to include an exception. The cloud provider should not be obliged to refer the request to the customer when to do so would put the provider in breach of legal requirements.

2.5 Key points

In this chapter we have explored issues around identifying which is the relevant body of law to apply to a cloud situation. Key points are as follows.

♦ Given the cross-border nature of cloud, it may be difficult to identify which legal system will apply to any given situation. Disputes as to which law applies to a particular situation have already arisen, and will continue to arise.

♦ A cloud provider and a customer can choose which law is to apply to govern their contract. A provider will normally (in its standard terms) make a choice which is convenient to it (normally, of its own jurisdiction). This choice only impacts the relationship set out in the contract and does not remove the need to comply with more general rules applicable.

♦ Other legal principles (such as requirements to comply with sales promotion laws or liability to third parties) cannot be avoided by contract and any entity wishing to sell internationally will need a strategy to decide in which country it will be legally 'cleared'. A practical and risk proportionate approach is necessary.

♦ The US Patriot Act [6] has received much publicity, but the law enforcement agencies of many countries have wide powers to obtain data within the relevant borders. When putting data into the cloud, a customer risks that data being accessed not only by such agencies in its country, but also in the provider's country.

3 Information security

3.1 Introduction

Survey after survey indicate that security of data or information is the biggest worry of customers contemplating moving to a cloud environment. They have an understandable fear of putting their data into the hands of a third party.

The fear customers have, say cloud providers, is often misplaced. No IT infrastructure is perfectly secure. Any corporate network, and therefore the stable of servers a potential customer enterprise might itself operate in a traditional IT department, is connected to the internet. This leads to the risk of malicious attack by hackers. No body of employees is completely trustworthy. There is always a threat of breach of protocol by employees (even assuming that the enterprise does have robust processes). Whilst there is no denying that the customer is losing direct control, the best placed people to navigate the risks are often the cloud providers whose job it is to keep data secure and who have a massive commercial incentive to keep abreast of the latest security developments and the latest solutions to the ever-changing security threats. There is of course much truth in this, certainly for the larger providers with reputations to safeguard. Cloud security is still in flux and it remains to be seen whether the smaller cloud providers achieve and maintain respectable levels of security. What is certain is that security will become a factor in the competition in the market, both in respect of what security is in place and also in respect of how open a provider is willing to be in relation to that security when confronted by customer queries.

This chapter explores aspects of the various security issues that arise in the cloud. We make no pretence of comprehensively dealing with the technical issues around security (and existing standards); these are topics worthy of their own books and reference should be made to specialist texts. However, we do introduce the security standards to which providers are claiming adherence in order to reassure customers. We discuss the legal obligations in this area, including issues such as due diligence and audit. Lastly, we discuss liability issues which arise when security goes wrong. Some of the issues discussed here are very closely linked to other issues covered elsewhere in this book. For example, when the data being entrusted to the provider is 'personal data' or the customer is a regulated financial services company then the regulatory overlay of data protection rules (discussed in chapter 4) or financial services regulation (13.2) come into play. Reference should also be made to 11.8 where we deal with contractual issues around liability generally.

3.2 Security breaches – some examples

There have already been some high-profile security incidents involving cloud services. As will be seen from the examples which follow, all of which were widely reported in the press, some arise as a result of technological errors and others because of malicious action by hackers.

3.2.1 Sidekick

Sidekick is a smartphone marketed by T-mobile. In the usual way, the device can store user data such as contacts, calendar entries, to-do lists and photos. However, unusually, the data was stored on servers in the cloud and not on the devices themselves. The servers are operated by Microsoft. In October 2009, the servers failed, data was lost, and users of these phones could not access their data. It was initially believed that the data was permanently lost. As a result, various legal claims were fairly promptly launched against both T-Mobile and Microsoft alleging that the companies had been negligent in looking after data. Microsoft later announced that the data had all been recovered. Microsoft then claimed that it was not a loss after all, simply an 'outage'.

3.2.2 Gmail

Google has not been immune to cloud service problems. Gmail is a free webmail service provided by Google (and a high profile example of a cloud application) and used by both consumers and businesses. Since it became available to the public in 2007, Gmail has experienced a number of outages. On 24 February 2009, Google's Gmail service went offline for about 2.5 hours affecting the service's 113 million users worldwide. During this time users could not access their Gmail accounts and were left seeing only an error when trying to login. However, Gmail's IMAP (Internet Message Access Protocol) service continued to work during this time allowing users to send and receive emails from devices such as the iPhone. The outage was caused by a routine maintenance event in one of Google's European data centres where new code, designed to try and keep data geographically close to its owner, caused another data centre in Europe to become overloaded and the problem spread across its data centres. It was quickly dubbed by bloggers as 'the great Gmail outage of 2009'.

Another outage occurred on 1 September 2009 resulting in the service being down for approximately 100 min although users could continue to send and receive emails using POP (Post Office Protocol) and IMAP during this time. It was reported in the press that the outage was caused by overloaded routers, triggered by a routine configuration change which added more router load than expected.

3.2.3   Google Docs

In March 2009, Google discovered a bug which caused some Google Docs users to share their documents without their knowledge. The documents were only shared with people with whom the user had already shared documents rather than the world at large. Google took immediate action when it found the error by stripping all sharing privileges on the affected documents and notifying the affected users that they would need to re-share their documents. It said that the problem only affected 0.05% of documents stored on the Google Docs site.

3.2.4   Google China

In January 2010, Google announced that it had detected a highly sophisticated and targeted attack on its corporate infrastructure originating from China which resulted in the theft of intellectual property from Google. The initial attack occurred when a company employee visited a malicious website. Due to a security hole, this caused the employee's browser to download an array of malware to their computer automatically and transparently. Google believed that the primary goal of the attackers was to access the Gmail accounts of Chinese human rights activists but they were only successful in accessing two accounts and in particular only the account information rather than the contents of emails.

3.2.5   Twitter breach

In 2009, a hacker reportedly broke into a Twitter employee's personal Gmail account using the password recovery feature that sends a reset link to a secondary email. In this case the secondary email was an expired Hotmail account which the hacker simply registered then clicked the link and reset the password. The hacker then read the employee's emails to guess the original Gmail password successfully and reset the password so the Twitter employee did not notice the account had changed. The hacker then used the same password to access the employee's emails on Google Apps and was able to download sensitive company information from emails and, particularly, email attachments. He then took over the accounts of at least three senior executives which enabled him to access more sensitive data. The hacker then used the same username/password combinations and password reset features to access AT&T, MobileMe, Amazon and iTunes, among other services. A security hole in iTunes gave the hacker access to full credit card information in clear text. He also had control of Twitter's domain names at GoDaddy. At this point, Twitter had absolutely no idea they had been compromised. The hacker then forwarded hundreds of pages of confidential Twitter documents to websites, including TechCrunch, which in turn published some documents and referred to others.

3.2.6   Hotmail breach

In October 2009, Microsoft confirmed that thousands of users of Windows Live Hotmail had their usernames and passwords posted on a third-party site. According to Microsoft, this information was likely to have been swiped in a phishing scheme and was not a breach of internal Microsoft data.

3.3   Due diligence

3.3.1   Introduction

Any entity outsourcing control of their data to a third party (whether cloud or otherwise) is always well advised to undertake some level of due diligence prior to signing the contract to ensure that security standards are as high as it is reasonable to expect given the commercial worth (or personal sensitivity) of the data. As will be seen later when personal data is involved or when the customer is operating in the financial services sector, due diligence in relation to security is not just commercial common sense; it is a regulatory requirement. Due diligence traditionally in an outsourcing situation might have involved site visits and detailed technical investigation of the organizational and technical processes in place. Clearly, this is easy to do when there is a specific data centre to be examined but less easy to do when a cloud is envisaged. In the cloud, a customer may simply have to resort to examining a provider's security policies.

The customer will want to be comfortable with what it finds out. However, this is not just an issue for customers. Providers are starting to appreciate that customers are becoming more security aware and recognize that they will increasingly need ready responses to these investigations.

3.3.2   Security policies

A typical security policy might cover the following areas.

a) Physical security – level of security of the servers including the policy on access restrictions.

b) Network security – including such things as the firewall technology to be deployed, and policies on employee access to customer data.

c) Server security – including how servers have been hardened against attack, policies for continual improvement.

d) Data segregation policies – clearly, physical segregation is not part of the model, but still need to include how logical segregation is to be achieved, user (client) authentication policies, etc.

e) Encryption – what algorithms and what strength; key management; what data is covered.

f) Back-up/Replication policies – how often this is to be done.

Under each of these headings there might be any of a number of different levels of description. Technical expertise is needed to assess the security offered. If that is not available in-house to a customer, consultancy services are available.

3.3.3 The customer's enquiries

The first and most important thing for the customer to do is to ask questions. This may take the form of a detailed questionnaire to be completed as part of a tender package, or meetings between technical staff, or even simply by studying public announcements on the security pages of the provider's web pages. The enquiries made will depend on the particular service. It is also important that full records are kept about the enquiries made and the responses received. This is particularly important for regulatory reasons as it serves as evidence to demonstrate that data protection, financial services or other regulations have been complied with.

It is impossible to be absolutely prescriptive as to what a customer should look into but a typical due diligence exercise for the cloud may include enquiring into:

a) who owns and controls the cloud infrastructure;

b) the deployment and delivery models;

c) the underpinning architectural framework;

d) the security controls in place;

e) the physical location of infrastructure elements;

f) the service provider's reliability reports (both in respect of security but also in respect of availability, the latter being essential to determine whether these meet the requirements of the business).

In the case of acquiring a cloud service which might be built upon a third party cloud service (as many SaaS solutions are), diligence should of course also be directed towards the sub-provider (who will, naturally, be the person who has actual possession of the customer's data). Adherence or certification to a particular standard of the SaaS provider, for example, is all well and good, but largely irrelevant if the data is held by a third-party subcontractor.

In undertaking a due diligence exercise, it is important that the customer insists upon detailed, technical responses to the questions. A customer should be wary of a cloud provider that simply replies with generalities such as 'We use encryption'. A response should elaborate: encryption to what standard? Is all data encrypted (both in transit and at rest)? How does authentication material get exchanged? What key management is in place? And so on.

3.3.4   The provider's response

In being asked these due diligence questions, how should a cloud provider respond? Of course, it wants the business, but much of the security it has in place is understandably confidential. Not only does such information perhaps constitute a commercial advantage, the disclosure of too much detail may compromise security. There is a natural reticence amongst information security experts to disclose.

Providers may well feel free to disclose the fact that they have a security policy and that it has had approval at the highest level (to the extent that is true). If the policy is an attempt to be compliant with an external standard such as ISO/IEC 27001 [11], that is certainly a good point to make – better still a certification to that effect. Beyond compliance or certification, however, a provider might well want to supply the customer with further detail. A customer may well want to see the full 'statement of applicability' (see 3.5.2) or otherwise some detail against each of the 11 'control clauses' set out in ISO/IEC 27002 [12] (see 3.5.3). A provider will of course want to stay clear of disclosing anything which is in fact proprietary or might in fact exacerbate security risks. A balance needs to be struck. Too much information can be dangerous as it might lead to liability issues if the information at some stage is no longer current. The less detail, the less likely the information will become dated.

Some providers are willing to provide more by way of security information (such as disclosing a level of detail around their architecture). However, before doing so they are likely to want to have the customer sign a confidentiality agreement (non-disclosure agreement or NDA).

PRACTICAL TIP

Providers should consider how much they need to disclose to reassure a potential customer as to the security measures in place. If confidential information is being disclosed, that should only be done under the umbrella of an appropriate NDA or confidentiality agreement.

Many customers will insist upon their own standard form of security questionnaire. Whilst this is all well and good from the customer's point of view, it does increase the burden upon the provider as part of the sales process. The economics of the cloud are dependent on it being easy to set up and use, and there must also be easy contracting. If too many customers send in too many questionnaires (all focussing on their own concern in their own form), this may detract from those economics. Providers fearing being inundated will need to educate their customers and this may well include being very open about security up front (rather than simply reacting to questionnaires).

PRACTICAL TIP

Cloud providers who find themselves bombarded with questionnaires might look at being more open on their websites. FAQs on security might be a useful tool.

3.4 Introduction to security standards

Given the difficulty of undertaking physical diligence, more and more customer reliance is likely to be put on an assessment as to whether a cloud provider adheres to a particular security standard. Of greater comfort still is when the adherence is certified by a third party (in particular, one that is accredited). A detailed summary of the various standards is outside the scope of this book, as is a discussion of how cloud providers might obtain certification against them. Nonetheless, a description of the major standards will be useful to those navigating legal aspects of the cloud. Compliance with and/or certification to these standards will often be cited by providers. A cloud customer needs to understand whether such compliance or certification is sufficient for it to satisfy its own commercial needs and risk appetite (as well as its regulatory and compliance obligations).

There are a number of international standards which (either directly or indirectly) tackle the security of IT systems or the management of information security. Whilst none focus on cloud, they are of general application and many (in particular, the ISO/IEC 27000 series and SAS 70 [13], both of which we discuss further on) are applicable to the cloud.

There are many benefits to a cloud provider of implementing sensibly-chosen security standards. First and foremost, it can itself be more confident that it is approaching the issue of security in a robust manner. Second, it can demonstrate that confidence to its customers. This will go some way to bridging the fear mentioned previously that too much control is being given to a provider over such important assets. Thirdly, it may provide some defence to claims for breach of regulatory compliance requirements, including the obligation to use appropriate technical and organizational means to safeguard security set out in data protection rules. To illustrate one aspect of this latter benefit, the UK Information Commissioner's Office has powers to issue fines for certain serious breaches of UK data protection rules (which we will explore more fully in 4.9.3). Amongst other things, the power arises if the data controller knows that there is a serious risk and has failed to take reasonable steps to prevent it. In its guidance on these powers, the Commissioner has stated[6] that is more likely to consider that the data controller has taken the required reasonable steps if it has implemented any relevant code of practice and an example of this (expressly mentioned) is if the controller can demonstrate compliance with ISO/IEC 27001 [11].

3.5   ISO/IEC 27000 series

3.5.1   Introduction to the series

The ISO/IEC 27000 series comprises information security management standards published jointly by the International Organization for Standardization (ISO) and the International Electrotechnical Commission (IEC). They were derived from an earlier BSI series (BS 7799 [14] and BS 17799 [15]).

The series for present purposes has two main components. First, ISO/IEC 27001 [11]: a standard that provides a specification for information security management systems and sets out a foundation for third-party audit and certification. It aims to ensure that information security management is established and maintained through a continual improvement process. It is possible to get third-party certification (by accredited organizations) against this standard.

> **PRACTICAL TIP**
>
> It is important for a customer to note that a cloud provider claiming to comply with ISO/IEC 27001 is merely self-assessing. This is very different from being certified against the standard.

---

[6]   Information Commissioner's guidance about the issue of monetary penalties prepared and issued under section 55C (1) of the Data Protection Act 1998, 12 January 2010 [16].

The second principal component in the series is ISO/IEC 27002 [12] which establishes the guidelines and general principles for initiating, implementing, maintaining, and improving information security management in an organization. Many cloud providers claim that they are 'compliant with' ISO/IEC 27002, but this is not necessarily very meaningful. As with claiming compliance with ISO/IEC 27001, that would simply be a self-assessment (and indeed there is no third-party accredited certification for this as there is for ISO/IEC 27001).

In addition, there are a number of sector specific standards in the ISO/IEC 27000 series, either already issued or in the process of being approved. These include ISO/IEC 27011 [17], which provides guidelines for telecommunications organizations, and ISO 27015, still being developed, which sets out security techniques and guidelines for financial and insurance sectors.

3.5.2 ISO/IEC 27001

ISO/IEC 27001 [11] provides a model for establishing and operating an information security management system (ISMS). By following this standard, any organization can adopt in a controlled fashion (and continually monitor and improve) processes to improve information security (in particular, the preservation of confidentiality, integrity and availability of information). It is possible to be certified against this standard (see 3.5.4).

This standard is designed for use by all types of different organizations and for different aspects of their processes. In order to be in compliance, all requirements set out in the standard should be addressed. However, given the potential for application by all types of organizations for different types of processes, there is scope for much variety in the contents of ISMSs and as to how the various requirements are in fact met, depending on such things as type and size of organization and risks faced.

Where a cloud provider claims adherence to ISO/IEC 27001, a customer will be concerned to explore two separate issues. Firstly, is the scope of the ISMS relevant to the cloud solution under consideration? Secondly, how has ISO/IEC 27001 been applied in that ISMS?

Taking these two issues in turn. In going through an ISO/IEC 27001 compliance project (whether ultimately certified or not), the organization will have first defined the scope and boundaries of the ISMS. Accordingly, the first thing for a customer to do when presented with a statement that the provider is ISO/IEC 27001 compliant is to satisfy itself that the scope of the ISMS said to be so compliant is in fact relevant to the data it will be entrusting to the cloud provider. A provider being ISO/IEC 27001 certified in relation, say, to the ISMS operated by its HR department (for its own personnel data) will not be of much comfort to the customer.

Likewise, as another example, a compliance scope relating to data centres located within the US will not be helpful if the customer's data is not to leave Europe.

PRACTICAL TIP

Where a provider claims adherence to ISO/IEC 27001 (or certification to it), the customer should understand the scope of the ISMS and ensure the cloud solution it is considering acquiring is properly covered.

Ensuring that the scope of ISMS covered by the compliance statement is in fact relevant to the cloud offering being contemplated is not enough for the customer, however. A provider will have had many choices to make in implementing an ISMS even when it is properly compliant with ISO/IEC 27001. Whilst third-party certification (see 3.5.4) will go some way to giving an assurance that sensible decisions have been made, a customer may well want to be directly satisfied that the controls actually in place are adequate and may want to explore some detail around those controls.

ISO/IEC 27001 sets out (in Annex A) a list of 133 control objectives and controls, which originate from ISO/IEC 27002 [12] (see 3.5.3).[7] Not all of the control objectives and controls will be relevant in any particular situation and so ISO/IEC 27001 permits the exclusion of an objective or control provided the exclusion can be justified. In summary, an organization can exclude the application of a control objective or control whenever it addresses risks the organization can accept, are not relevant, or can be passed onto others such as customers or suppliers. The assessment of which control objective or control can be dispensed with is undertaken with reference to the organization's documented risk assessment and risk treatment profile (which it sets itself).

The application of a control objective or control (or reasons for its exclusion) should be set out in a statement of applicability (SoA). In essence, therefore the SoA is a record of which of the various control objectives and controls in ISO/IEC 27001 Annex A have been applied (and how they have been applied) and which have been dispensed with. A certified provider would have had the SoA assessed and the decisions made by the provider will have been challenged. If there is no third-party certification, a customer will likely be more interested in this level of detail.

---

[7] The ISO/IEC 27000 series is in the process of being updated. One of the points of discussion is the removal of Annex A.

Where a provider claims adherence to ISO/IEC 27001, a customer relying on this should consider reviewing the statement of applicability. This is more important when there has not been an independent certification of compliance.

As mentioned in 3.3.4, however, a provider may well wish to resist full disclosure of the SoA if it does contain detail which is in fact proprietary or which might in fact exacerbate security risks.

3.5.3 ISO/IEC 27002

ISO/IEC 27002 [12] is a code of practice for information security management or, in other words, an information security standard. It is designed to complement ISO/IEC 27001 [11] by setting out many of the controls that can be utilized within an ISMS to help achieve certification under ISO/IEC 27001. The standard is structured by reference to 11 security 'control clauses' further split into 39 security categories. Each of the 39 categories contains an objective for the particular control stating what is to be achieved and then one or more controls (a total of 133) that can be applied to achieve that objective. The standard then provides for detailed information to support the implementation of the control and meeting the control objective.

The 11 main control clauses (set out in sections 5 to 15 of ISO/IEC 27002) are:

a) Security policy

An information security policy document should be approved by management, and communicated to all employees and relevant external parties. The policy should be reviewed regularly.

b) Organizing information security

This control requires the establishment of a management framework to initiate and control the implementation of information security within the organization. It also requires the maintenance and control of security when dealing with external parties; that, when doing so, a risk assessment is carried out; and that controls should be set out in an agreement.

c) Asset management

Responsibility for the security of any asset should be clearly set out. Information should be appropriately classified so as to ensure an appropriate degree of security is applied to it.

d) Human resources security

Security responsibilities should be addressed prior to, during and after employment. Adequate screening should be stipulated. Responsibilities should be defined for employees. Training should be provided and a formal disciplinary process should be established. Responsibilities should be in place to ensure an employee's exit from the organization is managed, and that the return of all equipment and the removal of all access rights are completed.

e) Physical and environmental security

Information processing facilities should be housed in secure areas, protected by defined perimeters, with security barriers and entry controls. They should be physically protected and commensurate with the identified risks. Equipment should be protected from physical and environmental threats and the electrical supply and cabling infrastructure safeguarded.

f) Communications and operations management

This clause is one of the most substantial in the standard. It sets out requirements (amongst other things) in each of the following areas:

i) that operational procedures and responsibilities for all information processing facilities are established;

ii) for appropriate monitoring of agreements with third parties;

iii) for advance planning and preparation of resources taking into account projections for future capacity requirements;

iv) that there is protection against viruses and malicious code;

v) for back-ups;

vi) for the secure management of networks, including any additional controls to protect sensitive information passing over public networks;

vii) that there is physical protection of media;

viii) that exchanges of information and software are only on a formal exchange policy, carried out in line with exchange agreements. Information in transit should be protected;

ix) (for e-commerce activities) that consideration is given to the security of online transactions and the integrity of information published;

x) that systems should be monitored and security breaches should be recorded.

g) Access control

This is another important section and includes requirements that:

i) access to information, facilities and business processes should be controlled on the basis of business and security requirements;

ii) formal procedures are in place to control the allocation of access rights to systems and services;

iii) users are made aware of their responsibilities for maintaining effective access controls, including in relation to passwords and the security of their equipment;

iv) access to networked services is controlled, and that the security of the network should not be compromised including by ensuring appropriate interfaces exist with external networks;

v) access is restricted to operating systems;

vi) access is also restricted to application systems;

vii) engaging in mobile computing and teleworking is secure.

h) Information systems acquisition, development and maintenance

This control requires that:

i) security requirements of information systems are identified at the requirements phase of a project and documented as part of a business case;

ii) appropriate controls should be designed into applications;

iii) a policy should be developed on the use of encryption and that a key management process should be in place;

iv) there are secure controls on access to system files and program source code;

v) project and support environments are strictly controlled;

vi) technical vulnerability management is implemented.

i) Information security incident management

This control requires that formal event reporting and escalation procedures for security breaches are in place, as well as responsibilities and procedures to handle events once they have been reported.

j) Business continuity management

A business continuity management process should be implemented to minimize the impact on the organization and recover from the loss of information assets to an acceptable level through a combination of preventive and recovery controls.

k) Compliance

A requirement that the organization complies with relevant legal requirements (including as to security and data protection), that it regularly reviews its compliance with its own security standards, and that it maximizes the effectiveness of and minimizes interference from any audit process.

3.5.4 Certification

Customers of any company who are dependent on the provider keeping proper security of data (or other assets) are free to take on trust a statement that they keep data secure to an appropriate standard (whether ISO/IEC 27001 [11] or another). Any such statement (if untrue) may well have legal consequences. This would certainly be the case if the statement is part of a contract. Nonetheless, in many instances a customer does not need simply to rely on such a statement. ISO/IEC 27001 (for example) has a mechanism for certification by a third party. The third party will audit the controls in place and then (if it is found that compliance has been achieved) certify as much.

PRACTICAL TIP

A customer should not simply rely on a statement that a cloud provider adheres to a standard on security. Rather, a customer should ask for evidence of independent verification or certification.

Certification against ISO/IEC 27001 is provided by a number of bodies both accredited and unaccredited, including the British Standards Institution (BSI). In the UK, the United Kingdom Accreditation Service provides 'accreditation' to organizations (such as BSI) wishing to provide the service to clients who want to have their compliance with a standard certified. A public register is kept of the certified organizations.[8] An increasing number of cloud providers are on this list.

PRACTICAL TIP

A customer should ensure that the certification is by a body of standing, ideally (but not essentially) an accredited body.

---

[8]   http://www.iso27001certificates.com/

To obtain certification against ISO/IEC 27001 is no mean feat and a real measure of the seriousness to which the cloud provider takes security. Indeed, there are many consultancies in the market who provide services to companies to get them to the standard where they can be certified. Ever increasing numbers of organizations are becoming certified and there are a number of reasons for this. First, certification is increasingly being required by customers. Secondly, enterprises feel a competitive pressure to get certified; their competitors have it, so they need it, too. Lastly, in the cloud environment, as a result of difficulties in permitting audits by customers, certification is one way of perhaps allowing customers to comply with the monitoring requirements required by regulation such as data protection law.[9]

A company relying on its intended cloud provider having certification should certainly ask to see all documentation relevant to it (including the full certificate issued and perhaps the underlying documentation (such as, with ISO/IEC 27001, the statement of applicability).[10] We mentioned in 3.5.2 that when a customer undertakes its own diligence in relation to ISO/IEC 27001 compliance it needs to ensure the scope document covers the relevant part of the organization. A similar consideration applies here.

> **PRACTICAL TIP**
>
> A customer should ensure, when relying on certification by a third party, that the scope of the certificate includes that part of the organization which is relevant to the solution the customer is acquiring.

3.6   SAS 70

3.6.1   SAS 70 is not a security standard

The Statement on Auditing Standards No. 70 (SAS 70) [13] is a standard developed by the American Institute of Certified Public Accountants (AICPA). Many (especially US-based) cloud providers are claiming to be audited to SAS 70 standards. Further on we examine the extent to which customers can take comfort from such a claim.

Although often referred to (in particular by cloud providers) as a security standard, SAS 70 is in fact an accounting process for an audit setting out standards for fieldwork, quality control and reporting. It can be used to audit many different types of controls and not only security controls or security management controls. Whatever the sphere of application, it says nothing about the substance of any controls or requirements; it only sets out how those controls should be audited. In particular,

---

[9]   See 5.5.

[10]   Although see the considerations of confidentiality mentioned in 3.3.4.

even if an organization's security controls are said to be compliant with (or more accurately, audited against) SAS 70, the standard says nothing about the security in place. SAS 70 is not a technology or security standard, it is an auditing standard.

> **PRACTICAL TIP**
>
> SAS 70 is not a security standard and cloud customers should take very little comfort from a statement that security at a provider is said to be SAS 70 compliant. Further enquiries should be made.

3.6.2 Auditing customers

The starting point is that an audit will be taken (in accordance with SAS 70 [13]) of an entity's control objectives and control activities. The auditor will then issue a 'service auditor's report' at the end of that process. Any organization could be subject to an audit requirement; that is, not only a cloud provider but also a user of cloud services. When a customer is subject to an audit in relation to its controls the audit will have within its scope a requirement to also look at the customer's use of service providers (and that includes any cloud provider as well as more traditional data centres or outsourced service providers). If a service (as is likely) impacts upon the customer's own controls, then the auditor as part of its responsibilities will also want to check the internal controls of that provider.

As, naturally, a service provider will have many customers, it would be incredibly wasteful to have all the auditors of all those customers separately examine controls of the service providers. The SAS 70 structure allows this waste to be avoided. A service provider can – of its own initiative – obtain its own SAS 70 audit which should also satisfy its customer's auditors.

3.6.3 Two types of reports

There are two types of service auditor's reports under SAS 70 [13]. A 'Type I' report sets out the provider's description of controls on a specific date and an opinion on whether that description is fairly presented and suitably designed to achieve control objectives. The controls themselves are not tested. A 'Type II' report contains all that is in a Type I report but also includes detailed testing of the provider's controls over a specified period (a minimum of 6 months) and therefore contains the auditor's opinion as to whether the controls were operating reasonably effectively during the relevant period.

When examining a cloud provider's statement that it has been audited to SAS 70, it is important for customers to:

- ask for the actual report;

- ensure it is a 'Type II' report; and

- examine the controls that are in place and have been described and commented on.

3.7 Contractual issues around information security

In this section, we explore a number of issues that arise in contracts for cloud services relating to security and data.

3.7.1 Contractual security schedule

The contract should set out an obligation upon the provider to comply with a particular security standard. It could be in general terms (such as, 'the provider will use reasonable efforts to keep data secure') but it would be better, as far as the customer is concerned, to set out some level of detail about what in fact will be provided. This would often be in the form of a security schedule.

Any customer, particularly one that is new to cloud computing, may attempt to insist (at least initially, in the earliest stage of negotiations) that the provider complies with the customer's own security policy. This is especially true of a more sophisticated customer, who may have its own in-depth and detailed security policy, which might be generally applicable across the enterprise, approved at the highest level, and not easily departed from. Indeed, customers with the highest level of information security policies may have dedicated teams and units whose sole role is to audit and vet their critical suppliers from an information security viewpoint. Such customers will need much persuasion to depart from their own policies.

A provider is likely to make a number of points in response. First, its service enjoys the benefits of cloud (low cost, elasticity, on-demand availability) precisely because it is a standard offering, perhaps in a multi-tenanted architecture. As such, the provider is not able cost-effectively to tailor its security policy for specific customers. If one customer insists upon, say, 256-bit symmetric key encryption for data in transit when the standard offering is 128-bit, the provider has the option of adopting the higher standard for all customers or of diverging the offering so that this insistent customer's needs are fulfilled whilst the others remain on the different standard.[11] None is ideal. The first option requires the expenditure of money which may not be necessary or useful for other customers. The alternative detracts from a proposition of the offering – to keep customers on the same playing field. Secondly, the provider of course is the expert in data security, or at least should be. If the provider, to continue the previous example, considers that 128-bit encryption is adequate for the purpose of this particular offering, given that the customer has decided to entrust its data to that provider, the customer might reasonably be expected to trust the security standards that are recommended. This is not to say that the customer should do so blindly, however. The customer does need to ensure that the policy is robust. The customer that is so well versed in security matters that it sets its own higher standard is more able to assess the provider's proposition. (And it is not inconceivable that some education takes place with the customer looking again at whether its own more stringent policy was indeed necessary.)

3.7.2 Rights to audit

A customer might insist upon a contractual right to audit the security of the data by undertaking a physical visit to the data centre. Such a right is of course very common in a managed services or outsourcing agreement, where there are dedicated servers or even dedicated premises for a particular customer, and only a 'single-tenancy' instance of the system. However, in a cloud environment, this presents difficulties.

First, it is not always clear where the data and servers are. In a true virtualized cloud environment the data could be anywhere, and indeed the location could be changing frequently and continuously. Accordingly, in practice, it is often not likely to be possible for a customer to inspect the security of its own data. Secondly, an audit of the provider's systems will necessarily involve an inspection of the systems of all other customers in the same installation. And what is good for one customer is likely to be equally applicable to others. A customer insisting upon a real, physical audit of data security might be reminded that the infrastructure is a shared one and that if it was agreed for them, they might have to agree such rights for all customers and that is something which this customer may not welcome. Thirdly, unless there is actual internal access to the systems, all that is really being inspected by a physical audit is physical security to the premises and the servers themselves.

---

[11] A further option, which may well emerge, is for a stratification to occur where different levels of security are available at different prices, although the point remains that these are always going to be 'standard' offerings in any case.

3.7.3 Constraints on location of data

A customer may well, for reasons explored elsewhere, wish to put contractual constraints on the location of data. Most vendors will want to have complete flexibility. Some vendors recognize the restrictions of the regulatory environment (such as restrictions on data flows outside of Europe where personal data is involved)[12] and are willing to give that assurance (perhaps for additional fees). Some of the major IaaS providers, for example, will tell their European business customers for at least some of their products that data will reside only in European server farms. It may well be important for a European customer to have this type of assurance.

If it is not possible for the cloud provider to give its European customer an assurance that data will remain in Europe, then, as discussed in chapter 4, one of the various mechanics to legitimize that transfer for the purpose of overcoming that restriction may need to be put in place.

> **PRACTICAL TIP**
>
> If data is to flow out of Europe, a customer should seek a contractual assurance from its provider that the mechanism chosen (if any) will be kept in place; for example, that the provider will remain in the US Safe Harbor.[13]

3.7.4 Provider liability for data

One of the most difficult issues to address in a cloud contract is the issue of the provider's liability for data. Data could be lost (in the sense of being deleted or irretrievably corrupted) or the security of data could be breached (in the sense of it being inappropriately disclosed to or accessed by third parties). Both issues are frequently dealt with together in the contract. A provider will often in its starting standard terms present carefully crafted language allowing it to avoid any or most liability for data. This may be acceptable to the customer if the data is not critical, if it is backed-up and if there is little risk of liability to third parties (such as under data protection legislation).

On the other hand, such a stance may be unpalatable to a customer. First, the purpose of the cloud service might well be as an alternative (and perhaps only) storage solution. Secondly, the customer might find itself with a very large bill for rectifying a problem which was not of its own making. To explore further this issue it useful here to briefly summarize some of the possible consequences of a

---

[12] See chapter 6.
[13] See 6.3.

hypothetical data breach and to discuss what types of loss the customer might suffer (and therefore seek to pass onto the provider).

a) Notification costs

The customer may want to notify individuals who are the subject of the data that the security of data has been breached. There is not (at present) a general obligation under UK law to do so (see chapter 7), but nonetheless there might be a desire to do so and indeed in some circumstance the Information Commissioner would recommend that it is done as best practice. The US experience, under their comprehensive notification laws, shows that this can be very costly, as notices must be prepared in accordance with legal requirements, which differ between states.

b) Assistance to individuals

Companies that suffer a breach will be faced with concerned customers. Help desks might need to be set up in order to deal with enquiries and reassure customers. There is a burgeoning industry of security experts who will assist. The cost of this might be significant.

c) Compensation to individuals

There might be financial damage suffered by individuals (for example as result of identify theft, fraud on their bank accounts and so on). These individuals will seek redress against the customer (not the cloud provider with whom they have no contract and may not even have knowledge of).

d) Damage to goodwill

There might be damage to reputation following a catastrophic breach so that custom is lost. This type of claim is notoriously hard to prove in court, but it might be possible if sales or share prices plummet.

e) Data might be lost or corrupted

If data is 'only' lost or corrupted, and not compromised, some of the costs just mentioned would not arise. However, there might be two types of claim here: first, the cost of reconstituting the data and, secondly, the financial consequences of not being able to use the data or of relying on wrong data.

A starting point for many providers is to exclude liability for loss which is of a purely financial type (such as damage to goodwill, inability to use the data, lost profits, and so on).[14] It is difficult for a customer to persuade a provider to move from its usual stance in relation to these types of losses. Where there might be movement, however, is in relation to 'direct' types of losses such as the cost of

---

[14] See also 12.2.

reconstituting the data (where it is the provider's breach of contract which caused a loss or corruption) or the cost of notifying individuals and setting up help desks. It might also be possible to have the provider take the financial consequences of claims brought by individuals against the customer (and this is normally covered by an indemnity against the claim).

Whatever is in principle recoverable, it will still likely be subject to a contractual cap on liability.[15]

PRACTICAL TIP

A customer needs to look very carefully at liability language. It is not uncommon for there to be an absolute exclusion of liability for 'loss of data' sometimes hidden in a more general liability exclusion provision.

3.8　Key points

In this chapter we have explored issues around information security. Key points are as follows.

◆ Information security and confidentiality is a big concern for customers. Security breaches have already occurred and will continue to occur.

◆ A customer entrusting their data to a cloud service will want to get some comfort (before contracting) that the provider addresses security in a sensible fashion. It may seek to do so by undertaking a due diligence process. Alternatively, or in addition, it may rely on a claim by the provider that it complies with a recognized standard.

◆ A due diligence process will involve the presentation by the customer of a list of questions and a response to that by the provider. Cloud providers are beginning to pre-empt the process by providing more information on their websites.

◆ As part of the diligence process a cloud provider will be concerned not to disclose trade secrets which are its competitive advantage or which if disclosed compromise the integrity of its security.

◆ The ISO/IEC 27000 series of standards addresses information security management and includes a certification process in relation to information security management systems (ISO/IEC 27001 [11]). Certification when achieved is a real measure of commitment by a provider. However, a customer should not rely on certification without at the very least checking that the scope

---

[15]　See also 12.3.

of the ISMS covered by the certificate includes all aspects of the cloud solution the customer is considering acquiring.

- The statement of applicability required by ISO/IEC 27001 sets out how each of the control objectives and controls that the standard requires the organization to consider are applied (or why they have been excluded). A customer should consider reviewing this (although the provider may be reluctant to disclose it for reasons of confidentiality).

- A customer should be comfortable that any external certification body is properly competent (and accreditation gives some assurance in this direction).

- SAS 70 [13] is a standard often mentioned (as an encouragement) by cloud providers (especially those based in the US). However, it is not a security standard (nor an information security management standard – such as ISO/IEC 27000 series); it is only an auditing standard. The cloud provider is free to set whatever controls it wishes and the audit describes those controls and the objectives they are intended to achieve.

- A SAS 70 'Type I' reports only the controls (chosen by the entity) and the objectives. The 'Type II' reports on the auditor's test of the controls. Given the lack of prescription as to the controls to be included in any information security system, great care is needed by a customer in relying on the existence of even a Type II report. Any report will certainly need careful scrutiny.

- Irrespective of any compliance with any external security standard, the contract should nonetheless contain a contractual agreement as to the standard to be applied to the customer's data. Given the 'standard' nature of the service (and its multi-tenancy aspects), it is unlikely that a cloud provider can agree to modify its standard security controls to adhere to any required by a specific customer, at least not without additional cost.

- A right for the customer itself to audit security arrangements may be irrelevant or inappropriate in a cloud situation given a possible lack of certainty as to the location of the data and the fact that servers will in any case be shared with many customers.

- Whatever the security standard agreed to, a cloud provider will seek in its contractual language to limit liability (or exclude it in entirety) if anything should go wrong. A security incident will likely impact all its customers, and that will inform its attitude to limitation language.

4   Data protection: basics

4.1   Introduction

One of the principal legal issues that arise in cloud computing is that of data protection law. Data protection legislation governs the treatment of certain types of information, broadly, information about individuals, known as 'personal data' in the legislation. These laws aim to impose minimum standards on those handling such information with a view to protecting the privacy of the individuals involved. It is inevitable, in most instances, that in providing cloud services the provider will be handling personal data on behalf of the customer. The UK data protection regime (set out primarily in the Data Protection Act 1998 (the DPA) [16]) will be a prominent legal issue in any cloud provision.

Given the fundamental importance of this issue, it merits introducing some of the underlying data protection principles before applying them to the cloud scenario. This chapter therefore commences with such an introduction.

4.2   The basic structure of data protection law

UK data protection law stems from the European Data Protection Directive [1] (the 'Directive'). As is usual, once the European Union has adopted a directive the UK (in common with other member states of the EU) has to 'transpose' those directives into its national law. In theory, therefore, there should be much commonality between the data protection regimes across the EU. However, as the member states have some discretion as to how to implement directives, there are 27 different implementations of this Directive. Some member states have 'gold-plated' the requirements (which set minimum standards). Other member states, such as the UK, have changed little substantively and adopted a more minimal approach. This variety of approach, coupled with the fact that each country has its own enforcement regime and court system interpreting the rules, can (and does) lead to inconsistency in the interpretation of the rules. To avoid too much inconsistency between what the different member states are doing and saying on common problems, the Directive set up an institution to provide guidance: the Article 29

Data Protection Working Party (the 'Working Party'). There are 27 members of the Working Party: the principal data protection regulators in each of the member states. The Working Party issues opinions and other papers. It does not however authoritatively interpret the law, which is a function reserved for the national courts with the European Court of Justice as ultimate adjudicator on issues of interpretation of European law including directives.

It is important to introduce the Working Party as it provides much guidance on the fundamentals of data protection law, some of which will assist businesses using or providing cloud services to determine either how particular data protection requirements will apply to their situation or (equally importantly) how the regulators might apply those rules to the cloud. It is to be expected that at some stage in the not-too-distant future, the Working Party will indeed consider cloud and issue some guidance on how it sees cloud being reconcilable with businesses' data protection obligations.

We commence with some fundamental definitions.

4.3   Personal data

The DPA [16] (and the Directive) apply to the processing of 'personal data'. 'Data' is information that, broadly, is stored electronically. This not only includes information that is within what one might consider to be a traditional 'database' – although that certainly is covered – but also any information in any electronic document. (Certain manual files are also within the definition but that is outside the scope of this book.) 'Data' is wide enough to include manual documents that are scanned into electronic form, CCTV footage, photographs uploaded onto photo sharing sites (of course, cloud services) and so on.

'Personal data' is any data 'which relate to a living individual who can be identified (a) from those data, or (b) from those data and other information which is in the possession of, or is likely to come into the possession of, the data controller'.[16] There are two parts of this definition that cause difficulties.

- 'Relating to'

  To be personal data the information must 'relate to' an individual. This captures the idea that not all information which may be connected with an individual is necessarily covered by the rules. The issue becomes: when is the connection between the information and the individual sufficiently close so that data protection rules are engaged?

---

[16]   Section 1(1) of the DPA [16].

- Identification

  The information must relate to an 'identified' or at least 'identifiable' individual. A name and address, NI number, passport number or other standard identifier is not necessary. Difficult issues arise in the technology world: when is an individual 'identifiable' in a world of IP addresses (which some argue only identify computers), RFID tags, cookies tracking behaviour, and so on? What happens if the data is anonymized? (Answer to this latter question: data protection rules no longer apply.)

To explore fully the nature of the debate on these concepts is outside the scope of this book. Regulators generally take a very expansive view of these definitions so that, essentially, most cloud services will involve the processing of 'personal data' and so if they have a UK (or European) element, the data protection rules will likely apply. By contrast, the UK Court of Appeal, in the case of *Durant* v *FSA*,[17] has taken a narrower view requiring that the information should 'focus' on the individual or at least be 'biographically significant'. The UK's view is not shared by other member states and is seen (outside the UK) as controversial.

PRACTICAL TIP

In practice, any data which refers to an individual (even indirectly through key-codes, IP addresses and the like) has the potential to be deemed to be personal data (by some regulators) and so cloud users should (except for the clearest cases, such as pure financial data or statistical data) consider the potential application of data protection laws.

The DPA makes a distinction between personal data and sensitive personal data. Sensitive personal data is personal data which consists of information as to a person's racial or ethnic origin, political opinions, religious beliefs, whether he or she is a member of a trade union, his or her physical or mental health, his or her sexual life, and his or her alleged commission of a criminal offence or related proceedings.

The individual (to whom the data relates) is referred to as a 'data subject' in the legislation.

4.4 Data controllers and processors

4.4.1 Introduction

Data protection law in Europe distinguishes between the concepts of data 'controller' and data 'processor'. Broadly, the controller 'owns' the data, and the

---

[17] 2003 EWCA Civ 1746. See: http://www.bailii.org/ew/cases/EWCA/Civ/2003/1746.html

'processor' is an agent handling the data for the controller. More specifically, the Directive defines controller as: 'the natural or legal person, public authority, agency or any other body which alone or jointly with others determines the purposes and means of the processing of personal data'.

A processor is: 'a natural or legal person, public authority, agency or any other body which processes personal data on behalf of the controller'.

'Processing' is given a wide meaning. It includes maintaining, recording or holding data, retrieving or using data, disclosing the data or the information, or carrying out any operations or set of operations on data (which – in the end – covers almost any activity). Manipulating personal data through a cloud service will be processing that will engage the DPA [16].

The interpretation of these concepts plays a vital role as they determine the responsibility for compliance with data protection rules and how the individual data subjects can exercise their rights in practice. As will be seen further on, a data controller has statutory responsibilities to data subjects and is subject to scrutiny of the regulatory regime and ultimately sanction through the courts; the processor has no such responsibility or real scrutiny. The controller (and not a processor) is also liable for any damage to data subjects which might arise out of breaches of its statutory obligations. It is of course possible for a controller to ensure (by means of a well drafted contract) that the processor takes the ultimate financial pain due to the processor's failures, for example by means of an indemnity from the processor to the controller. However, the regulatory burden and the initial primary target for any compensation claim will even then fall upon the controller.

Accordingly, determining whether or not an entity involved in the processing is a controller or processor is fundamentally important. On the face of it these terms seem fairly clear. A business owns the data and is therefore a controller; it entrusts the data to a service provider who must therefore be a processor. This is especially so in the cloud. It is tempting to take the view that a cloud customer will be the controller and the cloud provider a processor in relation to any of the customer's data which is placed into the cloud service. Unfortunately, regulatory activism show that the terms are not what they seem and there has been and continues to be much uncertainty in relation to how those terms are to be interpreted.

4.4.2 SWIFT

The SWIFT case from 2006 challenged the view that a service provider was always a data processor in relation to its customers' data and showed that this view was too simplistic. The Society for Worldwide Interbank Financial Telecommunication ('SWIFT') is a member-owned cooperative which conducts payment processing activities for the financial world. SWIFT transports messages between financial institutions. Each SWIFT message contains personal data, including the names of the beneficiary and the ordering customer of a payment transaction. SWIFT had two data centres: one in the EU, the other in the US. All messages processed in one centre were automatically stored and mirrored in the other centre.

Although not a cloud service, there are some features of the service which are cloud-like: the service is distributed, data (messages) are stored in multiple data centres of an indeterminate location, and the service is usable on a standard and highly scalable basis by its customers. SWIFT considered itself to be a data processor acting for banks and that the banks were the only data controllers.

In June 2006, it came to light that, since the aftermath of 9/11, SWIFT had been subpoenaed under US anti-terrorism law to provide certain US agencies with personal data collected and processed by the SWIFT network for international money transfers. In September 2006, the Belgian data protection authority issued an opinion affirming that SWIFT's processing activities were in breach of data protection rules. A little later, in November 2006, the Working Party agreed [18]. SWIFT was found to be not a processor, as it always professed, but a controller. In reaching this view, the Working Party considered that:

• it was irrelevant that SWIFT in its contracts referred to itself as a 'subcontractor' or processor;

• SWIFT had taken on specific responsibilities which go beyond those incumbent on a processor;

• SWIFT determined what personal data was processed and determined both the 'purpose' and the 'means' of the processing by developing, marketing and changing the service, for example, by determining standards as to the form and content of messages, all without reference to the users;

• SWIFT decided on the level of information that is provided to the financial institutions in relation to the processing;

• SWIFT also provided added value services, such as the storage and validation of personal data and the protection of personal data with a high security standard;

• SWIFT determined the security standard and the location of its data centres;

• SWIFT (not its members) decided to comply with the US subpoenas. It also took the initiative to negotiate with the US authorities (without informing the financial institutions concerned).

These actions were those of an antonymous controller, not those of a processor.

The view expressed by the Working Party is certainly controversial. All service providers (cloud or otherwise) determine their own security standard, the functionality of the service provided, the contracts to which they wish to be bound (either to its customers or to its suppliers) and the location of data centres, and these are all features identified by the Working Party as relevant to it reaching its view. Whilst it is true that determining such things is the determination (at some level) of the 'purpose and means' of the processing, as referred to in the definition, many argue that something more is needed.

Whilst SWIFT was subject to a subpoena under US law, it is important to remember that the situation could well have arisen within Europe – most countries have powers for the authorities to investigate terrorism and criminal activities. (The UK, for example, has the Intelligence Services Act 1994 [8], Police Act 1997 [9] and Regulation of Investigatory Powers Act 2000 [7])[18] This illustrates another controversial aspect of the regulators' views. Any service provider, located anywhere, may find itself under legal compulsion to give up data in its possession; and that alone – surely? – cannot make the provider a 'controller'.

4.4.3 Recent regulatory guidance

The resulting uncertainty on the meaning of 'controller' prompted the Working Party to issue an opinion [19] on that question in February 2010. The opinion did not discuss cloud, but its views are nonetheless important. The crucial aspect of the definition is to identify whether a cloud provider makes a 'determination' and then whether that determination is of the 'purposes and means of processing'.

The Working Party helpfully recognize that the Directive gives a margin of manoeuvre to a data processor; it is allowed some influence on purpose and means without promotion to the category of 'controller'. According to the Working Party, the questions that need to be considered are 'why the processing is happening and what is the role of possible connected actors like outsourcing companies: would the outsourced company have processed data if it were not asked by the controller, and at what conditions?'

Both the Working Party in this opinion, and the UK Information Commissioner in earlier guidance,[19] make it clear that determining 'purpose' is more important than determining 'means'. Determining 'purpose' would always trigger the qualification as a controller, but determining the 'means' would imply control only when the determination concerns the 'essential elements' of the means. Put another way, the Working Party states that it is possible that the technical and organizational means may be exclusively determined by a data processor (as might be in the case in many cloud services), but that would not make it a controller.

---

[18] See chapter 2 for further details.
[19] ICO, *The Guide to Data Protection* [20], paragraph 29, page 29.

Whilst some of this is reassuring, it is all rather abstract, and there is still much scope for debate as to when the means determined by the processor are 'essential elements' or not. The Working Party suggests that these include the determination of questions such as 'which data shall be processed?', 'for how long shall they be processed?', 'who shall have access to them?' – all factors, again (although they do not discuss cloud), that are normally determined primarily by a cloud provider. One feature of the SWIFT decision was that the provider determined the security standards. This is not really revisited with any clarity and so the position still remains unclear: precisely which decisions on security will make a cloud provider a controller? The Working Party does not attempt to address this issue in any comprehensive detail.

4.4.4 *Application to cloud computing*

Given the regulatory burden of being a controller, a provider will do what it can to avoid being deemed as such. Applying the guidance of the Working Party's Opinion, does the cloud provider 'determine' anything, and if it does is it a determination of the relevant kind; that is of 'purpose' or the 'essential means' of the processing? In any cloud customer/provider scenario, at some level, the cloud provider will determine at least some aspect of how (the 'means') the data is processed and indeed some aspect of why (the 'purpose') it is processed. Consider, for example, a SaaS vendor providing an online customer relationship management system for use by customers. It is the customer's data and there can be no doubt that the customer is a data controller, but is it the only one? The SaaS provider determines many aspects of the processing: the security to be put in place, the location of the servers, and so on – all factors of 'means'. At a higher level, the SaaS provider saw a market need to make its offering available in the first place – and so at some level sets the 'purpose' for the processing – easy access to data with all the 'cloud' advantages. Does making a determination to this type of extent make the provider a controller? The Opinion does make clear that some aspects of means can be delegated to the provider, but – in using the expression 'essential means' – leaves (frustratingly) unanswered precisely which aspects.

There are nonetheless some helpful comments which will bring comfort to at least some cloud providers hoping to avoid a determination that they are controllers. For example, the Working Party recognizes that specialist service providers (they give the examples of payroll service providers) will set up standard services and produce standard contracts to be signed by data controllers. The providers will remain processors (but then why does this rationale not apply to SWIFT?).

Nonetheless, in the end, it will not easily be possible for a cloud provider to be absolutely certain it will not be found to be a controller.

The following factors may assist a provider to avoid being characterized as a controller:

- Can the cloud provider give the customer choices as to any of the technical elements of the offering, such as encryption levels for storage and transmissions? Can these types of decision be built into the offering?

- It should not make any decisions itself (as far as the law allows) to cooperate with enforcement agencies in requests for its customer's data. It should always try to agree in its contracts with customers that it will pass such requests to the customer (again, where the law allows) for the customer to make the decision.

- It should give itself (in its contracts) very little discretion as to how and what it does with the data. For example, if the provider reserves the right – as some will do – to mine the data for its own commercial purposes (see 9.2) this will point towards the provider being a controller.

Even all this may not be enough and it is possible that regulators will increasingly take the view that a cloud provider (at least of a SaaS variety) will be a controller. Ultimately, a determination will depend on the precise service being offered.

If the provider is a controller, then difficult issues arise as to how the provider can comply with data protection rules in any case (Figure 2). There are obligations to provide information (including the identity of the data controller) to the data subject about the fact that the controller is processing the data.[20] But this is in the context of individuals who have no contact or contract with the cloud provider and the cloud customer is likely not to have informed the data subject of the outsourcing. There are similar difficulties with the data subject's rights to access data.[21] These consequences of a service provider being a controller have not yet really been fully considered by the regulators.

---

[20] Paragraph 2 of Part II of schedule 2 to the DPA [16], which implements Article 11 of the Directive.

[21] Section 7 of the DPA, implementing Article 12 of the Directive.

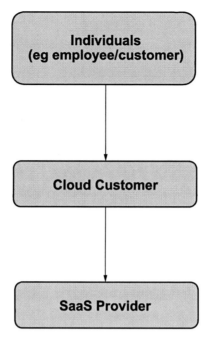

Figure 2. If the cloud provider is a 'data controller', how does the provider comply with data protection requirements with individuals with whom it has no contact or contract?

4.4.5 Multiple controllers

The definition of controller, in using the phrase 'which alone or jointly with others', clearly envisages that there might be more than one controller in relation to the processing of a set of data; a cloud provider and its customer could well both be a data controller. If this is the case, it leads to the possibility (recognized by the Working Party) that there might be joint and several liability for failures to comply with the rules. In other words, if there is a damages claim brought against the customer for a breach by the provider (or vice versa) both are equally liable. As far as the customer taking responsibility for the provider's defaults is concerned, this is really no different from when the provider is properly seen as a processor; the customer is always liable for the processor's acts.

PRACTICAL TIP

Cloud providers and their customers should agree in a contract who takes financial responsibility for the failure of the other to comply with data protection law. Reciprocal indemnities may well be appropriate.

4.5 Jurisdictional issues

4.5.1 Introduction

As discussed in chapter 2, one of the main issues with the cloud is that of knowing precisely where the data is and thus determining which legal regime would in fact apply. UK data protection law does have international reach. In particular, the DPA [16] applies to a data controller if:

- the data controller is established in the UK and the data is processed in the context of that establishment; or

- the data controller is established in neither the UK nor the European Economic Area but uses equipment in the UK for processing the data other than for the purposes of transit through the UK.

We consider these separately and apply these tests to typical cloud scenarios.

4.5.2 Established in the UK

Most easily, the DPA [16] applies if the data controller is established in the UK. The DPA says that the following are established in the UK:

- an individual who is ordinarily resident in the United Kingdom;

- a UK company;

- a UK partnership or other UK unincorporated association; and

- any person or entity that nonetheless maintains in the UK an office, branch or agency or a regular practice.

4.5.3 Established outside the UK

A non-European entity is subject to the DPA [16] merely if it is using equipment within the UK. Accordingly, and perhaps surprisingly, the DPA will also apply to data controllers that are outside of Europe but which use servers located within the UK (including those which are operated by service providers). Of course, if the controller never in fact 'comes into' the UK (i.e. if it never has an office or assets here), the data controller being within the jurisdiction of the UK for data protection purposes may mean nothing in practice except for a theoretical application of the rules, and a possibly theoretical transgression. The application of the DPA on such a theoretical basis is one thing; the ability of the ICO or courts to enforce the rules is another. Another point is that the ICO is unlikely to have any appetite to enforce against a non-UK controller merely within the DPA on the grounds that it is using the services of someone who has servers within the UK.

4.5.4 Application of jurisdictional rules to cloud

As has just been seen, the main test to establish the application of UK data protection law is the place of establishment of the data controller. An English customer therefore using the services of a cloud provider who is outside the UK, or who might be using servers outside the UK, remains nonetheless within the ambit of the UK data protection regime. Many non-European (in particular, US) entities selling cloud services to UK or European customers will come across these issues on a regular basis. They will be aware of the European rules, will be familiar with security requirements and issues around transfers of data out of Europe (discussed in chapter 6) and indeed may well have signed up (if they are in the US) to the 'Safe Harbor' scheme.

However, the fact that a non-European based customer might find itself within the European rules on the basis that it uses a cloud service within Europe will take many by surprise. Nonetheless, this is a likely consequence of the rule which states that using equipment within the EU is sufficient to found jurisdiction. A cloud provider within Europe (using equipment within Europe) will 'export' the jurisdiction of European data protection rules to its non-EU customers. However, if the European cloud service is in fact built upon a non-European IaaS service (where data is not held within Europe) then this rationale does not apply as there is no use of equipment within Europe. As can be seen, determining which law applies to data in the cloud can be very difficult indeed.[22]

4.6 The eight data protection principles

The fundamental requirement of UK data protection law is that a data controller must process data in compliance with certain guiding principles, the 'data protection principles', which are set out in a schedule to the DPA [16], and reflect provisions of the Directive (although they are not called 'principles' in the Directive nor grouped in the same manner). The schedules to the DPA also contain interpretative guidelines. Nonetheless the principles are set at a very high level and there is much scope for variation as to how they might apply in a particular context. Whilst the UK ICO provides useful guidance on many common issues, it has not as yet issued any guidance directly relevant to cloud services (of any description).

The eight data protection principles are as follows.

1. Data must be fairly and lawfully processed. This will not be satisfied unless one of the conditions set out in Schedule 2 to the DPA is met. In the case of sensitive personal data, one of the conditions in Schedule 3 must also be met. We discuss these schedules further on.

---

[22] It is not only the EU data protection law which causes these types of difficulties. See 7.6.2 for a discussion of how US data breach notification laws are also 'exported' to non-US providers.

2. Data must be obtained and only processed for the purposes specified.

3. Data must be kept adequate, relevant and must not be excessive in relation to its purpose.

4. Data must be accurate and up to date.

5. Data must be kept for no longer than is necessary.

6. The rights of the data subject must be respected.

7. Data must be safeguarded by technical and organizational measures against unauthorized access and loss or damage.

8. Data must be safeguarded and not transferred to countries outside the European Economic Area (EEA)[23] unless adequate safeguards are in place.

It is the last two principles that present the biggest challenge in a cloud environment, but the others remain important for both customer and provider alike.

4.7 Legitimization of processing

4.7.1 Personal data generally

The first data protection principle (that processing is fair and lawful) requires that one of the following six conditions (set out in Schedule 2 in the DPA [16]) must be fulfilled.

1. The data subject has given his consent to the processing.

2. The processing is necessary for the performance of a contract to which the data subject is a party.

3. The processing is necessary for compliance with a legal obligation to which the data controller is subject.

4. The processing is necessary in order to protect the vital interests of the data subject.

5. The processing is necessary for the administration of justice, or for other public functions.

6. The processing is necessary for the purposes of legitimate interests pursued by the data controller or by the third party to whom the data are disclosed, except where the processing is unwarranted in any particular case because of prejudice to the rights and freedoms or legitimate interests of the data subject.

The latter requirement (paragraph 6 of Schedule 2) is very important in practice and allows businesses to get on with unobtrusive activities. It is sometimes called

---

[23] The EEA is the European Union together with Iceland, Liechtenstein and Norway.

the 'balance of interest' condition or the 'legitimate interest' condition. It allows an activity to be undertaken if it is in the legitimate interest of the controller. Legitimate interests include such activities as marketing its services, organizing itself efficiently, outsourcing its operations (including into the cloud), and so on. The only caveat is that it must not prejudice the rights or interests of the data subject (and if it does, such prejudice must not be unwarranted).

4.7.2 Sensitive personal data

Sensitive personal data (see 4.3) have an extra level of protection under data protection rules. This includes information about racial or ethnic origin, political opinions, religious beliefs, trade union membership, health, sexual matters and information about crimes or alleged crimes. The main extra level of protection in relation to such sensitive personal data is that in addition to having to satisfy one of the requirements set out in Schedule 2 (applicable to personal data generally), a data controller has also to satisfy one of a number of more stringent requirements in Schedule 3. The following is a summary of the more important of the conditions in that schedule.

a) The data subject has given his explicit consent to the processing of the personal data.

b) The processing is necessary for compliance with employment law.

c) The processing is necessary to protect the vital interests of the data subject or another person (where consent cannot be obtained).

d) The processing is by a not-for-profit body existing for political, philosophical, religious or trade-union purposes and relating to individuals who are either members or have regular contact with the body.

e) The information contained in the personal data has already been made public by the data subject.

f) The processing is for legal proceedings, obtaining legal advice or for the purposes of establishing, exercising or defending legal rights.

g) The processing is necessary for the administration of justice, or for other public functions.

h) The processing is part of the operation of certain anti-fraud prevention organizations.

i) The processing is necessary for certain medical purposes by medical or other professionals under a duty of confidentiality.

j) The processing is for monitoring equality of treatment or opportunity related to racial or ethnic origin.

4.8   Notification to the Office of the Information Commissioner

A data controller is required to 'notify', to the Information Commissioner's Office, the fact that it is processing personal data. There are exemptions that apply to certain common activities which do not generally include any data protection concerns. The main exemptions can be summarized as follows.

a) Staff administration exemption. The processing is for HR purposes and is of data relating to staff of the data controller.

b) Advertising, marketing and public relations exemption. The processing is for the purposes of advertising or marketing the data controller's business and is of data of customers and suppliers.

c) Accounts and records exemption. The processing is for the purposes of keeping accounts of business dealings and is again of data of customers and suppliers.

Many small users of data, in particular, who do not do anything particularly adventurous or aggressive with personal data will fall within these exemptions. However, there is a serious doubt as to whether any of these exemptions will continue to apply to any data controller using a cloud service as each of these requirements includes the condition that there is no disclosure of the personal data to any third party. Using a cloud service is likely to be considered a disclosure.

PRACTICAL TIP

When moving to the cloud, even if a customer has previously relied on an exemption to notification, the position should be reviewed. A notification might now be necessary.

The other cloud issue likely to occur in relation to a cloud offering is around the details that the controller is obliged to file. The controller should file the names of the countries outside the EEA[24] to which the data is to be transferred.

PRACTICAL TIP

Unless there is a contractual commitment from the cloud provider that the data will remain within Europe or stay in a particular country, the registration should make it clear that the data could be anywhere in the world.

---

[24]   See footnote 23.

4.9 Enforcement

A feature of the UK implementation of the Directive, and in marked contrast to other European member states, is the relatively benign consequences of breaching the rules: there are very few criminal sanctions (and none directly relevant to a cloud situation), it is hard for individuals to claim compensation, and there are relatively limited powers for the regulator to fine.

4.9.1 Damages claims

An individual may be able to claim compensation if they have suffered damage or distress because of a breach of any of the requirements of the DPA [16] by the data controller. As mentioned previously, a controller has compliance responsibilities and a processor does not. Whilst there is some doubt as to whether or not a cloud provider will necessarily be deemed a processor (see 4.4), however it is characterized, a breach of security by the cloud provider resulting in the data subject suffering damage or distress will result in liability for the customer.

> **PRACTICAL TIP**
>
> Customers in the cloud may want to ensure that the contract contains a suitable indemnity in relation to any claim from a data subject as a result of wrongful processing (including breach of security) by the processor.

4.9.2 Enforcement notices

Enforcement of the DPA [16] remains primarily through administrative action by the regulator. The Information Commissioner has the power to serve 'enforcement notices' against data controllers breaching the data protection principles. These notices require the data controller to take or refrain from taking certain steps in relation to processing. If the Information Commissioner considers a customer to have breached the data protection principles in undertaking a cloud transaction, for example, it could serve a notice requiring the transgression to cease.

4.9.3 Monetary penalties

In 2010 a new power was given to the ICO to impose fines upon certain particularly grave breaches of the principles. A power to fine arises if (i) there has been a serious contravention of the data protection principles by the data controller, (ii) the contravention was of a kind likely to cause substantial damage or substantial distress, and (iii) either the contravention was deliberate or the data controller was (in a defined sense)[25] careless. If the contravention was not deliberate, there is no power to fine unless the data controller knew (or ought to have known) both that there was a risk that the contravention would occur and that such a contravention would be of a kind likely to cause substantial damage or substantial distress, and nonetheless had failed to take reasonable steps to prevent it.

It should be noted that there is no requirement that the damage or distress has actually occurred, only that the contravention was of a kind likely to lead to that damage or distress. Sloppy handling of security, through which no one has in fact suffered this type of loss, will be sufficient. This hurdle is high enough, but the legislation does not stop there. In order to fine:

- the ICO must be satisfied as to the matters just mentioned;

- it must first serve a 'notice of intent', which invites the controller to make written representations and certain timing details; and

- it may then (after expiry of time for the making of representations) serve a 'monetary penalty notice' setting out the penalty proposed.

The fine cannot be more than £500,000. The ICO has issued guidance[26] on how the power to fine will be exercised. The guidance deals with the circumstances in which the ICO would consider it appropriate to issue a monetary penalty notice, and how he will determine the amount of the penalty. This makes it clear that the ICO will take into account the sector and the size, financial and other resources of the controller and indeed that it is not the purpose of the monetary penalty notice to impose undue financial hardship on an otherwise responsible controller.

In relation to cloud services, security (the seventh data protection principle) is the most important to consider. Security is entrusted to the provider, but if there is a breach then the question of whether the ICO can fine the customer arises. The law is still young and there is as yet no reported instance of the serving of any penalty notice, let alone of any being levied in relation to cloud services. It thus remains to be seen how the ICO will apply these requirements. In particular, how will the requirement that there needs to be a 'deliberate' or 'careless' contravention of the security rules apply when security is entrusted to a cloud provider? Might a controller be fined because the provider was 'deliberate' or 'careless'? As discussed in 5.2, the requirement in relation to security when a processor is used is for the customer to ensure the provider gives 'sufficient guarantees' on security and for the customer to take 'reasonable steps' to ensure compliance with the security measures. If the controller has taken 'reasonable steps' to ensure compliance but

---

[25] Namely, the controller must have known that there was a risk of a contravention occurring and failed to take steps to prevent it.

[26] Information Commissioner's guidance about the issue of monetary penalties prepared and issued under section 55C (1) of the Data Protection Act 1998, 12 January 2010 [16].

despite taking those steps has failed to notice a deliberate or careless breach of the contractual security requirements by the cloud provider, it is arguable that there may in fact be no breach of security principle.

Whatever the compliance responsibility, a cloud customer will most certainly wish to be indemnified against any monetary penalty imposed upon it as a result of a breach by the cloud provider.

4.10   How does all this apply to the cloud?

In chapters 5 and 6, we consider the two principle issues arising from data protection law in the cloud context.

a) Are there any regulator requirements in putting the data into the cloud (irrespective of the issue of which country the data is in)?

The use by a cloud customer of a provider to process its data invokes issues around whether the provider is a processor or a controller. If the provider is a processor, the main compliance concern is for the customer to ensure it satisfies the seventh principle (to keep data secure). If the provider is a controller, the additional concern arises as to how that appointment can be 'fair and lawful' as required by the first data protection principle.

b) What are the requirements if data is not within Europe?

Inevitably, there is the possibility that data is transferred outside of Europe and so the eighth principle needs also to be considered, namely that personal data cannot be transferred outside Europe unless the data controller assures an adequate level of protection of the personal data.

4.11   Key points

In this chapter we introduced data protection, including some of the fundamental concepts and principles necessary to apply data protection law to the cloud. Key points are:

◆ Data protection law applies only to personal data. The definition of personal data is so wide that most (if not all) cloud implementations will involve to some extent or other the processing of this type of data by the cloud provider and so the application of data protection law.

◆ Data controllers have responsibilities under data protection law, but data processors do not. The tempting (and from a provider's viewpoint desirable) conclusion that only the cloud customer is a controller has been thrown into doubt by the analysis of the Working Party initially in relation to the SWIFT case.

◆ The more discretion a provider has in a contract to determine how the data is processed and for what purpose, the more likely that a regulator will take the view that the provider is also a data controller.

◆ The core of data protection law in the UK (and Europe) are the eight data protection principles. Security (the seventh principle) and transfer restrictions (the eighth principle) are particularly relevant in cloud computing and are discussed separately.

◆ The UK ICO now has a power to levy monetary penalties for certain serious breaches of data protection law. Data subjects also have a right to sue for damages for certain breaches. Even if caused by the cloud provider, a customer would be the target of any such regulatory action or data subject claim. A customer should include appropriate indemnities in the contract so that any liability that is properly the fault of the provider can be fully passed on.

5 Data protection: appointing a cloud provider

5.1 Introduction

We are discussing the situation where the cloud service involves the processing of 'personal data'. If the data is, say, purely scientific or financial or similar in nature, and does not relate to or identify any individual, then data protection rules will not apply. This chapter explores requirements which arise when such data is put into the cloud, independent of requirements which arise when data is transferred outside national borders; in other words, a UK company entrusting data to a UK cloud provider using only UK-based servers would have to address the compliance issues discussed in this chapter.

We discussed in chapter 4 the importance (and difficulty) of determining whether the cloud provider is a processor or a controller. Many cloud providers would hope that they would be considered to be a processor (and thus avoid various regulatory obligations). Nonetheless, following the Working Party's SWIFT decision and subsequent opinion [19], it is not possible to be absolutely certain that this will be the case in the eyes of regulators and enforcement agencies. We therefore have to consider the position under either possibility. The situation where a provider is properly considered to be a processor is considered in 5.2 and the situation where the provider is found to be a controller is considered in 5.3. Subsequent sections will detail considerations which apply however the provider is properly characterized.

PRACTICAL TIP

Given the present difficulty in determining with any certainty whether or not a cloud provider is a processor, and the risk of regulatory action if a wrong determination is made, a potential cloud customer intent on guaranteeing its compliance with the DPA [16] would do well to have regard to the possibility that the cloud provider is in fact a controller.

5.2 Cloud provider as a data processor

In this section, it is assumed that a cloud provider is a processor, and not a controller. The UK data protection rules deal with the appointment of processors only in one place: the security requirements set out in the seventh data protection principle (and explanatory text). The requirement is that data must be safeguarded by appropriate technical and organizational measures against unauthorized access and loss or damage. Leaving aside the appointment of a service provider, in order to decide what measures are 'appropriate' a controller is obliged to take into account the sort of data being processed, the harm that might result from its misuse and also the technology that is available to protect it. There is no requirement to buy 'best of breed' security; the DPA [16] makes clear that a controller may have regard to the cost of providing security.

The explanatory provisions around this principle deal only with processors generally and not cloud providers. Translated into cloud terminology, however, they require that when personal data is entrusted to a cloud provider, the customer must:

a) ensure the provider gives 'sufficient guarantees in respect of the technical and organizational security measures governing the processing to be carried out', and

b) take 'reasonable steps to ensure compliance with those measures'.

The security requirement is not to be considered as fulfilled unless there is a written contract in place (which is likely to include an electronic contract) and under that contract the processor is obliged to:

1. act only on instructions from the customer, and

2. require the provider to comply with obligations equivalent to those imposed by the seventh principle.

These requirements are on the face of it not hard to fulfil. The contractual language required by the DPA is language that a customer is likely to want in any case for commercial reasons – to only use the data on the customer's instructions (that is, for the customer's benefit) and to keep the data secure. The only potential difficulty is the level of security that is required by the seventh principle and which the DPA requires the customer to impose upon the provider. Having reached a view as to what is in fact appropriate, will the provider necessarily agree with the customer? We discussed the issue of the customer imposing its security requirement onto the provider in chapter 3.

5.3 Cloud provider as a data controller

If the provider is a data controller, then the act of the customer in putting the personal data into the hands of the provider is a disclosure to a third party and therefore an act of processing which needs to be 'fair and lawful' in accordance with the first data protection principle (see 4.7). Both the customer, in handing over that data, and the provider, in processing (which includes holding) that data, would need to comply with this principle and find a legitimizing basis (that is, satisfy one of the requirements in Schedule 2 of the DPA [16]). The customer is likely to be able to rely – in most circumstances – on paragraph 6 of Schedule 2: the 'balance of interest' test.

This test allows processing to be undertaken when it is necessary for the purposes of 'legitimate interests' pursued by the customer. It is certainly arguable that using a cost-effective, commercially sensible cloud service is a legitimate interest of the customer. The test also contains the proviso that the processing must not be 'unwarranted in any particular case because of prejudice to the rights and freedoms or legitimate interests of the data subject'. In order to undertake this balancing act it is submitted that the customer should undertake a risk assessment in relation to the cloud service which will involve a measure of due diligence into the offering itself, the legal status of the provider, the contractual protection for the data, and naturally the security measures in place. Only if the customer is satisfied in relation to such matters can it truly be sure that the rights of the individual are not being unduly prejudiced by the decision to put the data into the cloud. It should of course also put a written contract in place limiting the ability of the provider to process the data. In other words, the customer should undertake the same type of pre-contract exercise as it would take if the provider was considered a 'processor'.

5.4 Pre-contract due diligence

As we have just discussed, it is at least arguable that the level of diligence legally required to be made of the provider's circumstances by the customer is broadly the same whether the provider is truly a processor of the customer's data or rather a controller. And whether or not a legal requirement, it will clearly be commercially sensible from a security standpoint not to make such distinctions. In either case, there needs to be an enquiry into the legal position of the provider and the security position of the data.

PRACTICAL TIP

Whether the provider is a data processor or a controller, the customer needs to undertake some due diligence in relation to security, not least to satisfy its regulatory requirements.

A recap: the seventh data protection principle requires that 'appropriate' security is taken. The UK ICO makes it clear in guidance (again, not with specific reference to cloud services) that what are appropriate security measures will depend on all the circumstances. The customer should – before contracting with the cloud provider – consider the type of data involved, the potential harm which might arise for the individuals, and the available technology. The rules go further however than ensuring that the provider itself is robust in its security measures. ICO guidance makes clear (in the general outsourcing situation)[27] that the customer should take into account the legislation in place in the country where the provider is located (when the data centres are outside of Europe). The customer should consider whether the provider's country has any particular security risks associated with it, including whether there is any data protection legislation in that country and whether any other legislation may affect the security of the data. (We are not considering here the issue – which arises separately under the eighth data protection principle and we discuss in the next chapter – of how a customer can legitimize the transferring of data abroad. Having said that, some of the factors relevant to an assessment of the seventh data protection principle will also be relevant to an assessment of the eighth principle.)

We consider two possible scenarios.

a) The location of the servers is known, and they are known to be outside of Europe.

   The customer should take into account the legislation in place in the country where the provider is located, including any which might apply to the provider, such as the US Patriot Act [6] (see 2.4.2). Does this mean that because of the risks of such foreign laws, a US or other non-European cloud provider should be avoided? The law in most EU countries would probably not go that far. However, a recent report of a German data protection regulator (that of Berlin) states that it would violate German law to use a cloud with servers outside of Europe without the explicit consent of the data subjects.[28] The position from a UK viewpoint is not so stark. The UK ICO guidance in fact envisages outsourcing to non-European countries and there is no reason to suppose that the ICO would look dimly on a cloud provider simply on the basis of its location – at least when the destination country is known – provided that proper and compliant diligence has been undertaken and controls are put in place.

b) The location of the servers is unknown.

   Applying the ICO's guidance to this scenario is problematic. It requires some consideration of the laws in the destination country and if the location of the servers is unknown this cannot be done. To follow the letter of the ICO guidance to the extreme, therefore, it would not be possible to do this. However, this guidance was not written with cloud in mind, and it may be that future guidance will be more sympathetic to the cloud model and therefore less restrictive.

---

[27] ICO, *Outsourcing – a guide for small and medium-sized businesses* [21].
[28] Data Protection Officer of Berlin (Berliner Beauftragter für Datenschutz und Informationsfreiheit), Datenschutz und Informationsfreiheit Bericht 2008.

PRACTICAL TIP

A customer should ask the provider to identify where the servers upon which data will be stored are located.

5.5   Ongoing monitoring requirements

A further requirement of the seventh data protection principle is to take 'reasonable steps to ensure compliance with those security measures'. This is often interpreted to require the ability (which must then be included in the contract) physically to inspect the provider's facilities. If that really was a requirement it would make it well nigh impossible for any European customer to acquire cloud services when personal data are involved (at least in a lawful manner); so the issue is very important.

The ICO – again in the context of outsourcing generally – says simply 'you must choose a provider that you consider can carry out the work in a secure manner and, while the work is going on, you should check that they are doing this',[29] which implies (but does not expressly state) a physical inspection. In their more detailed and general guidance, they write that 'organisations should choose data processors carefully and have in place effective means of monitoring, reviewing and auditing their processing'.[30]

However, it is not necessarily the case that data protection compliance requires the controller itself to inspect and ensure that data is kept secure. We suggest an alternative approach. Although there is no official guidance as yet indicating as much, and certainly no enforcement action or other form of litigation, it is arguably possible that this could be fulfilled, for example, by having an external auditing of security, perhaps as part of standard certification.[31] This is not inconsistent with a sensible, pragmatic approach to such matters in a non-cloud appointment of a data processor. One of the reasons often cited to justify the outsourcing movement is that it leaves a customer to concentrate on core competencies, and the technology (whether processing of personal data or otherwise) is then left to a centre of excellence in that particular field. As such, it would seem strange to then assume that there is a requirement for the customer itself (which does not perhaps then retain internal technical competence) to audit security; how can it when to do so may well be outside its field of expertise? It might – on a correct reading of this compliance obligation – be sufficient for the customer to appoint an external consultant to audit and if that much is allowed, perhaps an external certification process would also suffice.

---

[29]   See footnote 27.
[30]   ICO, *The Guide to Data Protection* [20].
[31]   See chapter 3

5.6   ICO's views on cloud computing

The UK ICO has issued a code of practice on online data protection issues: *Personal information online Code of Practice* [22]. In this document the ICO takes a pragmatic view of cloud computing (although it has to be said that the guidance within this code is nowhere near as comprehensive as the more considered guidance on outsourcing generally already referred to previously). The code clearly envisages the possibility of lawful cloud use by an enterprise. It emphasizes that data should enjoy adequate protection wherever it is located. Whilst 'this raises compliance issues that organisations using internet-based computing need to address', the ICO is also pragmatic in this guidelines. It recognizes that despite 'the potential problems, there can be advantages for your company's back-up and security procedures if multiple copies of personal data are held in multiple locations'.

The ICO emphasizes the need to ensure that the customer does not relinquish control of the personal data or expose itself to risks that would not have arisen had the data remained under the customer's control in the UK. The code reminds companies to keep data encrypted during the course of transmission. A risk analysis should be carried out, which will include asking the types of diligence questions discussed throughout this book. Two areas for diligence enquiry specifically emphasized by the ICO are worthy of mention here:

- what assurances can the provider give that data protection standards will be maintained, even if the data is stored in a country with weak, or no, data protection law, or where governmental data interception powers are strong and lacking safeguards?

- can the cloud provider send the customer copies of its information regularly, in a standard format, so that the customer holds useable copies of vital information at all times?

5.7 Key points

In this chapter we have delved deeper into the data protection issues that arise when personal data is put into the cloud. Key points are as follows.

◆ A cloud provider might be either a data controller or a data processor under data protection law; and it may not be possible to be absolutely certain which is the case.

◆ Whatever the proper characterization of the provider, the customer (in order to satisfy its regulatory obligations) needs to undertake some due diligence in relation to security, to impose security requirements upon the cloud provider and to prevent the cloud provider from using the data for other purposes. These regulatory requirements coincide with commercial concerns in any case.

◆ The UK ICO will – on any investigation – want to see that a risk analysis in relation to the cloud solution has been undertaken. This should be documented.

6 Transfers of data to non-EU cloud providers

6.1 Introduction

We now consider the other principal issue for cloud structures under UK and European data protection law: the restriction on data flows out of Europe contained in the eighth data protection principle. It is important to bear in mind that the discussion in this section is separate from the discussion in relation to security in the seventh principle. There is overlap, of course, in that both compliance obligations will necessitate an assessment of security and may require an assessment as to the local laws that might impact upon the security.

Under the eighth data protection principle (reflecting Article 25 of the Directive) personal data may not be transferred outside the EEA[32] unless the data controller assures an 'adequate level of privacy protection', such transfers being subject to very limited exceptions. The rationale behind these rules, albeit perhaps difficult for non-Europeans to appreciate (especially when the laws of their countries are adjudged not to be 'adequate'), is logical: a data controller subject to the jurisdiction of the European rules and the safeguards imposed upon the personal data within Europe should not be able to send the data outside its borders without ensuring that an equivalent level of protection is afforded to citizens' privacy. Otherwise the protection offered to the privacy of its citizens is severely limited (it would fall away by the controller simply sending the data abroad); and indeed, it is not only the European member states which have such rules – most jurisdictions that have data privacy laws have such rules (the US, China and Japan being important exceptions). Whilst this stance may well be logical, however, the way that the European rules apply, and the bureaucracy attendant on putting in place compliance methods, is – in the view of many commentators (even regulators) – in serious need of modernization. The rules were set up when large-scale data transfers happened perhaps rarely and perhaps when it was clear that a certain set of data was in fact moving on a particular date from one destination to another – an analysis of

---

[32] See footnote 23.

'data flows' in a particular business, system or transaction was relatively easy. Of course, in the modern age where data can be anywhere, and indeed in many places simultaneously, and accessed from anywhere else with the greatest of ease, that type of analysis breaks down.

This restriction has proved problematic for many international businesses with a genuine need to share data throughout the world and has implications for many standard business activities leaving aside cloud computing. It impacts upon the freedom to send data amongst members of an international group, or even simply from appointing an outsourced service provider outside of Europe. It has obvious implications for cloud scenarios where the provider may not be within Europe, but the customer is.

We consider the impact of these rules, both from the cloud customer viewpoint (where they are attempting to comply with European data protection rules) and from the provider viewpoint (where they are trying to accommodate the customer's compliance concerns).

6.2   Countries deemed automatically adequate

So, the requirement is that the controller sending data out of the EEA (the 'data exporter') ensures that there is an 'adequate level of privacy protection' for the data. The Directive allows the European Commission to make a finding in relation to the adequacy of the protection offered by a specific country. Transfers of personal data to the countries in this 'safe list' would automatically meet the adequacy standard. The process involves an analysis of a foreign country's laws by the European Commission and then a public assessment made as to their adequacy. It is internationally controversial as by and large the European Commission will not find adequate laws which do not have about them the 'flavour' of the Directive. In other words, it operates in practice as a way of exporting European data protection sensibilities across the globe, even if that is not the main purpose for the rule.

At the time of writing, only a small number of countries have been the subject of adequacy findings (including Argentina, Canada, Switzerland, and Jersey, Guernsey and the Isle of Man). The US, of course the source of many of the most prominent cloud services, is a notable omission from this list.

Accordingly, if the cloud provider is in one of these 'adequate' countries, and can give an assurance that data remains in that country, no more needs to be done by the customer to satisfy the eighth data protection principle.

If a European controller is relying on the cloud provider being in one of the adequate countries, they should make sure that the data is transferred to (and remains in) that country and it is not simply the location of the provider's headquarters.

It will still be necessary to obtain a contractual promise from the provider to keep data in that country.

6.3 The US Safe Harbor

6.3.1 Introduction

The United States is not on the list of 'adequate' countries. The US does have often very stringent privacy laws but it takes a different approach to the EU. It has adopted a sectoral approach to privacy laws relying on a mix of legislation at a state and federal level. There are, for example, a number of federal laws in relation to specific sectors, including health data (HIPAA [23]), financial data (The Gramm-Leach-Bliley Act [24]) and child online data (COPPA [25]). At a state level there are robust data breach notification regimes (see further at 7.2). Nonetheless, the approach is not sufficient in European eyes given its lack of generality for protection of all classes of data across all sectors.

As a result many US cloud providers seeking to sell services into Europe are signing up to a scheme called the 'Safe Harbor'. This scheme was negotiated in 2000 between the US and the EU to overcome the general lack of 'adequacy' and a fear that the coming into effect of the new European data protection regime at the turn of the millennium would impact upon US–European trade. US entities (in any sector) can sign up to this scheme and commit themselves to complying with a set of data protection principles.

There are seven principles, backed up by guidance provided by the US Department of Commerce and a number of Frequently Asked Questions, that together broadly reflect the contents of the European rules. By complying with the Safe Harbor principles, US companies are deemed to have adopted an adequate level of protection for transfers of personal data to the US from EU member states. As such, if a US cloud provider is a member (for the relevant types of data), its UK customer can transfer data to the provider without fear of contravening the eighth data protection principle.

If a provider is a US entity, the customer should enquire as to whether or not the entity has self-certified as to Safe Harbor. A customer should confirm this independently by consulting the publicly available list and not rely on publicity material of the provider.

6.3.2   The mechanics of Safe Harbor

Joining Safe Harbor can be fairly straightforward. A US cloud provider would have to self-certify to the US Department of Commerce that it adheres to the Safe Harbor principles and make a public declaration of this adherence. Once accepted, a company is added to the publicly available Safe Harbor list.[33] Whilst there is no approval mechanism (acceptance being a purely administrative act), a joining provider should nonetheless ensure that its privacy policy is compatible with the principles and be prepared to make its privacy policy publicly available before going ahead with self-certification. A provider has to verify annually the implementation of its privacy policy (this may be by self-verification or verification by a third party). It must also file a self-certification letter once a year.

The Safe Harbor website includes contact details for handling complaints, requests for data access and other issues arising, the statutory body with jurisdiction to hear claims under US law, and the independent recourse mechanism available to investigate unresolved complaints in relation to that company.

Importantly, an entity can sign up to Safe Harbor for different types of data. It might do so for example in relation to its own internal data (such as HR data or data about its own customers – as opposed to data entrusted to a cloud service by a customer). As such, the customer wishing to rely on the provider being on Safe Harbor should ensure by confirming with the public list that the relevant data is covered.

A customer relying on Safe Harbor as a mechanism for permitting the transfer of its data outside of the EEA should confirm that the relevant data is covered by the provider's self-certification.

Despite its broad appeal, the Safe Harbor scheme has some drawbacks. US providers who wish to benefit from this scheme must take positive steps to comply with the seven principles. For instance, they must (at least if they are a controller)[34]

---

[33]   Available through http://www.export.gov/safeharbor/
[34]   See section 4.4

71

give notice to individuals of the purposes for which their personal data is collected and used. They must also disclose any onward transfer (i.e. a transfer to a third party or use for a different purpose) and give individuals an option to opt out of the onward transfer, which will make it difficult for a cloud provider using a third party data centre (for example, a company at the SaaS level acquiring infrastructure capacity from an IaaS supplier). More importantly, providers will need to be aware of the enforcement obligations.

6.3.3 How are the Safe Harbor principles enforced?

The 'enforcement' principle of the Safe Harbor principles (Principle 7) requires implementation by a provider of a suitable independent mechanism to deal with complaints or disputes and of a procedure for periodic verification of compliance with the principles. In addition, in relation to complaints, a company adopting Safe Harbor must either elect that a US self-regulatory organization is responsible for dealing with them, or it can elect that such complaints fall under the jurisdiction of the European data protection authorities. Companies are committed to remedying complaints in accordance with their findings.

The Federal Trade Commission (FTC) and Department of Transportation (DOT) have the right to file deceptive trade practices charges against a company failing to live up to its Safe Harbor promises. There remains much controversy as to how effective enforcement is for Safe Harbor. There has been no such charge brought against a member for failure to comply with the principles (although in 2009 charges were brought against entities who claimed to be on Safe Harbor but were not). This is despite a report by Galexia (a management consultancy) in December 2008 concluding that only around a third of the entities on the list in fact comply. In 2010, some German regulators were particularly critical of the scheme and pronounced that German companies should not merely rely on membership but should undertake proper checks as to compliance in relation to US recipients of their data.

As well as regulatory enforcement, there is scope for both the transferring data controller (the cloud customer) and the individuals who form the subject of the transferred data to make a claim for damages in relation to a breach of the Safe Harbor principles. To date no such claim has been made.

6.3.4 Limitations on the scope

Not all US entities are eligible to join. A fundamental requirement is that the entity is subject to either FTC jurisdiction or the jurisdiction of the DOT (US air carriers and ticket agents). Two important sectors are not within that jurisdiction: the US financial services industry (regulated for privacy by the Federal Reserve and others) and telecommunications carriers (subject to the jurisdiction of the Federal

Communications Commission). It is unlikely that many cloud providers are in these sectors.

A possible further limitation is whether there is proper coverage for HR data. Many of the companies who have signed up to Safe Harbor have done so for the purpose of sending human resource data to the US. However, there is some doubt as to whether it can be used for this purpose. Indeed, in 2004 the European Commission raised doubts over the jurisdiction of the FTC to enforce Safe Harbor with regard to transfers of employee data even though the Safe Harbor FAQs agreed by the Commission and US Department of Commerce expressly foresee the possibility of joining Safe Harbor for this type of data transfer. FTC jurisdiction is for deceptive trade practices (which would include the privacy aspects of the relationship between a business and its customers), but not for regulating the privacy aspects of the relationship between that business and its employees. Nonetheless, the fact remains that despite the doubts expressed in 2004 the scheme has continued to be used for the purpose of transferring HR data. Many cloud solutions will be used for the processing of employee data, and the absence of any regulator movement on this issue (and there has been none since the point was raised in 2004) means that, practically, this could prove a solution when the customer can be confident that the provider will keep the data in the US.

6.4 Standard clauses

6.4.1 Introduction

Cloud providers which are located in countries outside the scope of automatically adequate countries and which are not US Safe Harborites can avoid the data export ban and receive data from their European customers by signing certain standard forms of contracts (known as 'standard clauses') that will assure 'adequacy' for the purpose of the Directive. The Directive contains a mechanism by which the European Commission can approve standard forms of contracts between the data exporter in the EU and the data importer (that can be a processor or a controller) based outside the EU. These standard clauses are intended to provide self-contained adequate safeguards for personal data transferred. The original set of data controller to data controller clauses issued in 2001 ('Set I') were not widely used because they were considered too restrictive and commercially difficult to agree. An alternative and more business-friendly set was eventually adopted in 2004 and has gained much wider currency ('Set II'). A further set of standard contract clauses was issued in 2002 for use with processors (and these were replaced, due to widespread criticism of the original, in 2010). Each of the standard clauses must – to satisfy the regulatory requirement – be used in the precise form approved. Various detail (such as names and addresses of the 'data exporter' and the 'data importer' and the types of data) need to be completed. If other amendments are made they are no longer automatically considered to provide an adequate level of protection.

6.4.2 Standard clauses in the cloud

The use of any one of these sets of clauses (un-amended) would automatically remove any risk of non-compliance so that a European customer dealing with a cloud provider under a contract, which includes the clauses, can proceed; there should in theory be no additional requirements to fulfil. However, in practice many of the European regulators review the contracts stringently. Some countries require the standard clauses (as executed) to be filed and even approved prior to the initial transfer. Other countries, such as the UK, have no additional formality required. Indeed, when a compliance programme is intended to cover a number of European companies exporting under broadly the same arrangement, it is not uncommon for there to be inconsistency between the attitude of different regulators, for example some insisting that the transfer is best characterized as one to a controller, whilst others taking the view that the recipient is a processor. Given the difficulty in characterizing a cloud provider as controller or processor, it is easy to see how this inconsistency can arise in a cloud situation.

The standard clauses used will not of course replace the principal contract between the customer and a cloud provider; full commercial terms (including in relation to information security) will be needed. The clauses are in addition to those terms. The standard clauses chosen could be simply incorporated as a schedule to the main agreement or signed separately; the precise form does not really matter. As noted, however, whichever set is used, they cannot be amended (at least not without losing the automatic compliance with the eighth data protection principle which is the main benefit).

From a customer's perspective, persuading a cloud provider to sign one of the sets of standard clauses is attractive. And when it is used a customer will be largely free of any regulatory criticism. In the UK, certainly, there is no requirement to file the clauses with the ICO and the ICO will likely not take too much of an issue if a good faith assessment was made by a provider to use, say, the controller-to-processor clauses when in reality the proper analysis showed that the cloud provider was a controller (and so implying that one of the controller-to-controller sets should have been used).

PRACTICAL TIP

If a cloud provider is not within Europe and is not on the US Safe Harbor list, then a customer could request that the provider signs one of the sets of standard clauses.

From a provider's perspective, signing the contract has an advantage of satisfying its customer as to the customer's regulatory requirements. Nonetheless, a cloud provider may well hesitate to adopt this solution to the cross-border data flow issue. The standard clauses are contracts and can therefore be enforced both by its customer and by the data subjects (who are expressly given rights in the contracts to enforce at least some of the terms in certain circumstances). Whilst the accompanying main contract governing the commercial agreement between the parties will likely have limitation of liability language,[35] which would apply if the provider breached, say, the obligation to keep data secure, none of the different sets of standard clauses contain such provisions. This leads to the possibility of the standard clauses being used by a cloud customer to bring a claim against the provider larger than that which would have arisen under the main contract, thus 'circumventing' the contractual limitation language.

The main agreement could include liability exclusion or limitation language wide enough to cover not only liability under that agreement but also under any 'parallel' set of standard clauses. Whilst this works contractually, it is unclear whether that would be seen by the regulators and the courts as departing from the standard clauses in such a way as to prevent the eighth data protection principle from having been complied with. If the regulators or the courts did take that view, then the cloud customer will have been deprived of the benefit of having the standard clauses in the first place.

PRACTICAL TIP

A cloud provider outside of the EEA may wish to resist signing an EU approved set of standard clauses on the grounds that the liability position which arises is unacceptably inconsistent with the position which might have been agreed in the 'commercial agreement'.

The provider should consider drafting the main agreement to exclude or limit liability under the standard contract.

A customer should hesitate in allowing an exclusion of liability in the main agreement from applying to the standard clauses as it may mean it is not then compliant with the eighth data protection principle.

6.4.3 Onward transfers by the cloud provider

A criticism of all the standard clauses is that they lack any clear provision dealing with onward transfers or subcontracting by the data importer, that is when the receiving party in turn sends data onto some other entity. In modern outsourcing (let

---

[35] See 3.7.4 and chapter 12.

alone cloud) this is a fairly common situation. This lack of provision makes it difficult for a non-EU cloud provider to then entrust personal data to a subcontractor. A realistic scenario to illustrate these issues would be where a European customer contracts with a SaaS provider based in the US, but where the SaaS provider has built its service on an IaaS or PaaS offering of its subcontractor. The subcontractor will have possession of the data in its own data centres. This is considered to be an 'onward transfer' by EU regulators. If the customer has put in place one of the sets of standard clauses with its SaaS provider, the set needs to permit that onward transfer. Do the standard clauses allow this? The answer to this is not straightforward and in fact depends not only on whether the SaaS provider is a controller or processor (see 4.4), but also on the proper characterization of whether the subcontractor is either a controller or a processor. There are therefore four scenarios to be considered.

First, the SaaS provider is a controller and so too is the IaaS/PaaS subcontractor. Either of the two controller-to-controller clauses expressly permit the further transfer to another controller only if the data subject is given an opportunity to object (clearly, in a cloud situation, unrealistic) or if the other controller signs up to the same clauses. The customer therefore needs to ensure that the IaaS provider also has to sign contract clauses with it!

Secondly, the SaaS provider is a controller and the subcontractor is a processor. Whilst neither of the contracts expressly permits the onward transfer to a processor, Set II recognizes that the importing controller may indeed appoint a processor and no onward transfer issue arises (Set I is uncertain).

Thirdly, if the SaaS provider is a processor, the subcontractor cannot be a controller. The subcontractor cannot (at least lawfully) determine the means and purposes of processing if the main provider cannot to do so.

Lastly, if the SaaS provider is a processor, any subcontractor (as just mentioned) must also be a processor. Here, unless the SaaS provider is a US Safe Harborite or in an 'adequate' country, a customer will have to put in place the new (2010) controller to processor clauses, enabling the non-EU processor to appoint subcontractors. This is subject to very complex requirements including the following (in the context we are discussing).

a) The non-EU based SaaS provider must obtain its customer's prior consent in writing. This can presumably be obtained in the contract under which the cloud services are being provided. This is not without difficulty, however, as a SaaS provider may not want to publicize the fact that it is subcontracting.

b) Worse still, the SaaS provider has to send to its customer a copy of the contract under which any sub-processing takes place. Given that a SaaS provider is likely to want to keep confidential the commercial aspects of the arrangements with its subcontractors, it would be advisable to have two separate and parallel agreements – one dealing with commercially sensitive aspects and the other dealing purely with the 'data processing' aspects.

c) There is then also a requirement that a data subject be provided with a copy of the contract (at least the 'data processing' parts) if it is requested.

These four alternative possibilities can be summarized as shown in Table 1, which illustrates the position under the standard clauses when a SaaS provider subcontracts to either a IaaS provider or a PaaS provider.

Table 1. Are onward transfers permitted?

		SaaS provider	
		Controller	**Processor**
Subcontractor (IaaS/PaaS Provider)	**Controller**	IaaS/PaaS provider needs also to sign standard clauses with customer	N/A
	Processor	Permitted under Set II	Yes, but difficult

This leads to the conclusion that data protection compliance through contracts, when there is a hierarchy of different cloud providers whose services are built upon each other, is easier when the main provider is a 'controller' than when it is a 'processor', a strange state of affairs.

6.4.4   Onward transfers when subcontractor is in a different country

None of the sets of standard clauses have a requirement that the 'importer' keeps the data in a specified country. However, there is a requirement upon the importer in all the contracts to at least be aware of the country in which the data is stored. This is because it gives an assurance that it knows of no legal difficulty which might apply. Specifically:

a) in the controller-to-controller Set II clauses, the cloud provider gives an assurance that 'it has no reason to believe, at the time of entering into these clauses, in the existence of any local laws that would have a substantial adverse effect on the guarantees provided for under these clauses' and goes on to require the provider to inform its customer if it becomes aware of any such laws;

b) in the controller-to-processor clauses (the new, 2010 set), the cloud provider gives an assurance that 'it has no reason to believe that the legislation applicable to it prevents it from fulfilling the instructions received from the data exporter and its obligations under the contract'. Again, if it becomes aware of a change it is to inform its customer.

It is arguable at least that these assurances cannot properly be given if the provider does not know where the data in fact is.

Given the convolutions necessary here, it is tempting for any EU-based cloud customer to simply dismiss contracts as a suitable solution in the cloud space. However, in many member states (if not the UK) there are limited alternative mechanisms (unless the cloud provider is in Safe Harbor or in an 'adequate' country) and there can be serious sanctions for failure to comply. The UK permits a little more leeway as it allows the security of data to be 'self-assessed' by the controller itself (to which we now turn).

6.5   Self-assessment

6.5.1   Introduction

The 'self-assessment' approach to legitimizing transfers of data from member states to third countries is a valid approach in the UK (but not generally throughout the other member states). The approach is based on the premise that the data exporter should itself consider and make a judgement as to whether, in the particular circumstances of a transfer, that transfer is made to a country that can ensure an adequate level of protection. The DPA [16] imposes a direct obligation upon data controllers to ensure, and assess, adequacy of the protection of the data when it is transferred. In short, the data controller should approach the eighth data protection principle in the same manner as it approaches the other data protection principles. Just as it makes its own assessment as to whether or not processing is fair (first principle) or as to security measures to take (seventh principle), and so on, it too has to make its own assessment as to whether there is an adequate level of protection.

This compliance method can certainly be useful in a cloud situation. The approach has been endorsed (arguably, even encouraged) by the UK ICO generally and in particular for outsourcing, although there is no express mention of cloud in the relevant guidance. The UK ICO states in its guidance on data transfers[36] that if it is required to investigate a particular transfer, it 'will expect to see evidence that the data controller making the transfer has followed the approach and the various criteria set out in this guidance'.

---

[36]   This guidance comprises two separate documents: a legal analysis of the eighth principle 'The Eighth Data Protection Principle and international data transfers' (the 'UK Legal Analysis') and also a more business orientated paper containing general compliance advice for companies transferring personal data overseas (the 'UK General Compliance Advice').

6.5.2 Undertaking the analysis

The UK ICO's guidance on data transfers emphasizes that when a controller is considering whether there is an adequate level of protection it should take into account a number of factors. These include certain specific criteria related to the data itself such as the nature of the personal data, the purposes for which, and period during which, the data are to be processed, and any security measures to be taken. However, there is also a requirement to consider more general 'legal adequacy' factors in the destination country. Here a controller should consider the legal background in force in that country that will give protection to the data (even if not in the same way as in Europe), including any relevant codes of conducts and treaty obligations. Having said that, the UK ICO recognizes that it would be inappropriate for exporting controllers to consider such legal adequacy criteria exhaustively in the case of every transfer to a third country. Nonetheless, controllers are expected to be able to recognize countries where there would be a real danger of prejudice or where it is clear that the country in question does not provide any legal protection in relation to the exported data. The UK ICO has made it clear that he expects the data controller to take a more cautious approach in relation to any such transfer.

The UK guidance does not expressly deal with cloud providers. It does however deal generally with outsourcing, and there is no reason to believe that the approach (if not the result) set out in respect of this type of service should not extend to cloud services. In relation to outsourcings, the ICO makes it clear that the transfer would not normally present a problem from an eighth data protection principle standpoint, and that the parties do not, in fact, ordinarily have to put in place standard clauses:

> a data controller in the UK need not necessarily use these controller-processor[37] model clauses when entering into a contract with a data processor in a third country ... The model clauses are merely one method of addressing the requirements of the eighth principle and there are many other methods ... which may be more appropriate in the circumstances.

> ... In this respect, the Commissioner's guidance is that compliance with the seventh principle will go some way towards satisfying the adequacy requirements of the eighth principle (given the continuing contractual relationship between the parties and the data controller's continued liability for data protection compliance ...)[38]

---

[37] Note with reference to the discussion in 4.4 the assumption in this statement that an outsourced service provider will be a 'processor'.

[38] See footnote 36.

The reason for this is that, where such a transfer is made, the UK data controller exporting the data remains the controller and, as such, remains subject to the Commissioner's powers of enforcement. In effect, it remains responsible for protecting individuals' rights under the DPA [16] in relation to the overseas processing of the personal data by the data processor.

Of course, where there is a transfer to a data processor, wherever that processor is located, a data controller must still comply with the seventh data protection principle (security).

6.5.3   Self-assessment applied to the cloud

A cloud provider is simply one form of outsourced provider and it is submitted that there is no reason to assume that the ICO would take a dimmer view of that type of outsourcing; at least as long as the security, contractual and monitoring requirements are fulfilled. Indeed, that is the stance the ICO takes in the code of practice on online privacy discussed in 5.6; the ICO places no particular emphasis on standard clauses or Safe Harbor. However, as mentioned, the ICO would expect the cloud customer to make due diligence checks in relation to the provider and conduct some examination of the type of matters usually looked at in relation to adequacy. This aspect does present a potential difficulty. The types of matter which should normally be examined include aspects of the country in which the data processor is located and its security arrangements in that country – which clearly assumes that the data is where the provider is. It is only if such due diligence and analysis did not reveal any particular risks in relation to cloud service that this approach would satisfy the ICO in relation to adequacy.

> **PRACTICAL TIP**
>
> A cloud customer wishing to rely on self-assessment as its eighth data protection principle compliance method should, at the time of making the assessment, document that it has done so and the assessments made against each of the relevant factors.

If a cloud customer can be certain about where the data is, then a proper self-assessment taking into account the legal landscape in that country can readily be undertaken. However, this would be difficult to fulfil in a cloud situation where the location of the data is uncertain.

A non-EU-based cloud provider will likely be happy to rely on the customer's self-assessment as the eighth data protection principle compliance method. Under this method, the provider would accept no liability as it would do under the standard clauses (or under Safe Harbor). The liability would only be as set out in the commercial agreement with its customer.

6.6 Binding corporate rules

Yet a further method of legitimizing transfers of data outside of Europe is by having a set of so-called 'binding corporate rules' (BCRs) approved by the European regulators. These facilitate the international sharing of data between entities within the same group so immediately it is obvious that in an arm's length third-party provision of cloud services, they are just inapplicable. However, entities that are setting up a 'private cloud' may find this a possible solution.

The scheme involves the corporate group setting up an internal suite of documents setting out how the group intends to provide adequate safeguards to individuals whose personal data is being transferred to a third country. These must contain data protection safeguards no less than those provided for in the Directive. Setting BCRs can be a challenge because a corporate group must create legally-binding internal documents for the benefit of affected individuals, with one delegated company taking responsibility for the compliance of the whole of the group while the rest of the group is required to undertake comprehensive data protection audits. When all these internal steps are completed, the BCRs are submitted to one national data protection regulator (perhaps in the country where the organization has its EU headquarters). This, in turn, except for a fairly recent innovation, liaises with the other relevant national data protection authorities with the aim of getting approval by all the authorities concerned. An iterative process then takes place as comments are fed back to the lead authority and the organization. For the biggest groups of companies there may need to be formal approval from all 27 member states' regulators. The recent innovation is the creation of a mutual recognition scheme in October 2008 by the Article 29 Working Party which provides a 'one-stop' shop for BCR applications covering 19 member states.[39] Under the scheme, if one of the member countries (the lead authority) approves an application for BCRs, the BCR is automatically approved in the other member countries.

---

[39] Including France, Germany, Ireland and the United Kingdom.

Not surprisingly, BCRs have been criticized as offering a solution that is only really appropriate for the most sophisticated international organizations and, in particular, only for those that wish to share amongst their group and not externally. After an unimpressive start, BCRs have recently gained some momentum in the wake of standard 'checklists' and processes and the mutual recognition schemes. Since then large multinational companies such as Accenture, Atmel and Hyatt have opted for BCRs as their regime of choice for complying with the Directive. Companies such as these, provided that the BCRs cover the relevant type of data and that the BCRs apply to the particular offering, need do no more when putting their data into a private cloud (where the cloud provider is a company within that group).

6.7   Other derogations

There are other methods of transferring personal data to third countries. A transfer can take place without ensuring adequacy of protection by means of one of the methods just discussed if one of a number of conditions is satisfied including:

- the data subject giving his consent to the proposed transfer;
- the transfer being necessary for the performance of certain contracts between the data subject and the controller;
- the transfer being necessary or legally required on important public interest grounds, or for the establishment, exercise or defence of legal claims.

Consent is often discussed in this context, but is not without problems (a full discussion of which is outside the scope of this book). Whilst it is superficially attractive, consent must be given freely, be specific and informed and, where sensitive personal data are concerned, must also be 'explicit'. The Article 29 Working Party suggests that relying on consent may prove to be a 'false good solution', appearing simple at first glance but, in reality, complex and cumbersome. What if one of thousands of data subjects withholds consent? What if one data subject revokes their consent? For a European business outsourcing its data processing to a cloud provider, these are largely irrelevant.

6.8   Key points

In this chapter we have explored the additional data protection issues that arise when European personal data might be stored or otherwise processed outside of Europe. In particular we looked at the various methods for a data controller to satisfy the obligation to ensure that data is adequately protected. Key points are as follows.

- If data is sent to an 'adequate' country outside of the EEA (although there are very few of these), then no further issue occurs provided the customer can be sure the data stays in that country.

- A US cloud provider could be on the Safe Harbor list, and provided the certification is up to date and relevant to the data being transferred it is a good solution for the customer. The cloud provider however is at risk of action by the FTC (or DOT) if it breaches the principles.

- Standard clauses are another solution which generally work well from a customer's point of view. However, from a provider's point of view, it is at risk of accepting greater liability under the clauses than it ordinarily would like to. It is uncertain whether any liability under these standard clauses can be capped in the same way as liability can be generally in the 'parallel' cloud contract.

- A customer could 'self-assess' the adequacy of protection. In many situations, when (i) the data is not particularly sensitive, (ii) a sensible security diligence has been undertaken, (iii) proper contractual language is in place, and (iv) the cloud provider is a reputable company of substance in a country with a developed and sophisticated legal system, it will not be unreasonable for the customer to satisfy itself that there is adequate protection. There is however no guarantee with this method that a regulator would agree.

7 Data security breach notification in the cloud

7.1 Introduction

This chapter considers whether there are any requirements to inform individuals or regulators if there is a breach of security in the cloud.

It is all well and good to have a robust and substantive data protection law, which many countries (certainly, of course, in Europe) do have, but when those laws are breached and there is a danger of leakage of personal information to the potential detriment of the individual concerned, the issue arises as to whether there is a legal duty upon the data controller to notify the individuals concerned. These laws are generally known as 'data breach notification' laws and, as we will see, the position in the UK (and in Europe) is that there is at present generally no such obligation. Nonetheless, the data will be in the hands of a cloud provider who may be in a jurisdiction (notably the US) where there are such obligations. The issue which then arises is whether the provider itself might be subject to such a law when it is the provider's customer's data that has been compromised.

7.2 The US position

Given the prevalence of cloud services originating in the US it is important to appreciate a sense of the landscape there. The US has been in the lead in terms of passing data breach notification laws. The laws are currently at state level, with over 45 US states now having such laws in place. It is interesting that the US has done this given its different approach to data protection generally. Unlike in Europe, there is no general protection of an all encompassing class of 'personal data'. Instead, US legislation generally tends to be very sector specific with different legal regimes for each of health data,[40] financial data,[41] online data about children[42] and so on.

---

[40] The Health Insurance Portability and Accountability Act of 1996 ('HIPAA') [23] Privacy and Security Rules.

[41] The Gramm-Leach-Bliley Act ('GBL') [24].

[42] Children's Online Privacy Protection Act ('COPPA') [25].

The data breach notification laws differ from state to state. They are concerned only with specific types of data (different in each state). For example, California (the first state to enact such laws) initially enacted them for names and addresses together with at least one of the following: social security number, drivers licence/ID number or bank account details (only if a PIN or password was involved). Other states (now including California) have extended the laws to medical records and other types of data. Some states only require notification to their own citizens (not those of other states or non-US citizens). Moreover, they apply to any company (whether located within that state or indeed within the US or not) who holds the relevant data about one of the state's residents. In practice, however, data breach notification in the US seems to be given to all individuals who might be concerned irrespective of residency.

7.3 Data breach notification in Europe

There is no general data breach notification requirement in the Directive, although some individual member states (notably, Germany in 2009) have enacted such requirements. The UK, as yet, has not. However, there will shortly be such a requirement to those operating in the communications sector as a result of a recent amendment to the Directive dealing with privacy in the communications sector (the 'E-Privacy Directive' [26]). Provisions relating to data breach notifications in that sector should become law by 25 May 2011.

The E-Privacy Directive applies only to telecom companies and to ISPs. It does not generally apply to all activities on the internet. As a result of the changes, to be brought in by the amending Directive [27], it will provide (when it comes into effect) for notification of

> a breach of security leading to the accidental or unlawful destruction, loss, alteration, unauthorized disclosure of, or access to, personal data transmitted, stored or otherwise processed in connection with the provision of a publicly available electronic communications service in the Community.

In the event of such a personal data breach, the covered entity must, without delay, notify the relevant regulator about the breach. If the breach is likely to adversely affect the personal data or privacy of an individual then the provider must also notify them of the breach. However, where the data is encrypted, the provider is unlikely to be required to notify the individuals affected.

When the requirement to notify arises, the provider must at least describe the nature of the breach, provide contact points for further information, and recommend measures to mitigate the possible adverse affects of the breach. The notification to the national authority must, in addition to the above, describe the consequences of, and the measures proposed or taken by the provider to address the personal data breach.

7.4   ICO guidance on data security breach management

Whilst the UK has no express legal requirement of general application, the ICO has given guidance on when notification should occur.[43] This guidance came about as a result of a number of high profile security breaches (including the HMRC breach of 2007 when CDs containing the unencrypted data of 25 million families receiving child benefit were lost).

The guidance states that notifying individuals and organizations that a data security breach has occurred can be an important element in a breach management strategy. It recognizes that notification of a breach is not an end in itself. An organization should have a clear purpose when informing people, whether this is to enable affected individuals to take steps to protect themselves or to allow the appropriate bodies to perform their functions, provide advice and deal with complaints. The guidance suggests that a notification should at the very least include a description of how and when the breach occurred, what data was involved and what the organization has already done to respond to the risks posed by the breach.

In deciding whether or not to notify individuals, the ICO states that an organization should consider its legal and contractual requirements, whether notification will help it to meet its security obligations under the seventh data protection principle, if notification will help individuals mitigate the risk from the breach and the dangers of over-notifying. If there are a large number of people affected by the breach or very serious consequences, the ICO states that it (the ICO) too should be informed.

The nature of the breach will, according to the ICO, determine to a large extent who should be notified. The organization should consider notifying third parties such as the police, insurers, professional bodies, bank or credit card companies and trade unions. When notifying individuals the ICO states that an organization should always give clear and specific advice of the steps that they can take to protect themselves and what the organization can do to help them. Contact details of the organization should be provided to allow individuals to contact it for further information or with specific queries.

PRACTICAL TIP

Whilst the ICO's guidance is non-binding, the ICO will likely, when considering its enforcement powers, look more favourably upon a controller that follows the guidance than one who doesn't. Cloud customers (and providers) subject to UK law should have due regard to this guidance if there is ever a security incident.

---

[43]   ISO Guidance on data security breach management, 27 March 2008.

7.5 Specific UK sectors

7.5.1 Public sector

As a result of the many recent security breaches in the public sector, it is now operating a 'voluntary' data breach notification regime. Government departments and NHS organizations are required to notify the ICO in the event of a data breach. There is no statute creating this rule – it results from a report by the Cabinet Office 'Data Handling Procedures in Government' (the 'Report'), which followed the Data Handling Review commissioned by the then Prime Minister in November 2007 following the HMRC breach. The Report also gives the ICO the power to carry out spot-checks on government departments to ensure that they are complying with the DPA [16].

7.5.2 FSA and other regulatory regimes

Principle 11 of the Financial Services Authority (FSA) Handbook [28] requires a regulated firm to deal with its regulators in an open and cooperative way and to disclose appropriately anything relating to the firm that the FSA would reasonably expect to be told. Firms are required to notify the FSA of any significant failure in a firm's systems and controls. This would cover any serious data breach or where a security lapse indicates a breakdown of proper systems and controls. There is no specific requirement for firms to notify individuals but the FSA has said that it has the power to order companies to disclose details of a data breach to its customers.

In an FSA report on Data Security in Financial Services (April 2008) [29], the FSA said that consumers affected by a data breach have a right to know the enhanced personal risk they face so that they can take adequate precautions. It also stated that it is good practice for firms to inform affected customers of a data loss in writing, unless the data is encrypted or there is law enforcement or regulatory advice to the contrary. Firms should consider telling affected consumers exactly what data has been lost, give them an assessment of the risk and give advice and assistance to consumers at a heightened risk of identity fraud.

7.6 Application to the cloud

The issue of present concern is where the cloud provider has a security lapse under which its customer's data is compromised. Does either the customer or provider have a duty to notify the individuals concerned or the relevant regulators? There are two possibilities to consider: whether the law of the cloud customer requires notification and/or whether the law of the provider requires notification.

7.6.1   Obligations upon the cloud customer

Taking the first of these, as the cloud customer remains a data controller for the purposes of UK data protection laws, the fact that its provider has suffered the breach does not remove its obligations under the DPA [16]. Generally, as we have seen, there is no duty to notify (unless the controller is operating in the telecoms sector or a regulator such as the FSA requires it), but good practice suggests that the cloud customer nonetheless has regard to the UK ICO's guidance.

7.6.2   Obligations upon the cloud provider

The second possibility is where the provider is in a jurisdiction with data breach notification laws (say, California or other relevant US state). US law only applies to the 'owner' of the data and so cloud providers are not within the scope – the laws of the various US states do not regard a service provider generally as an 'owner' for this purpose. However, the typical US state law data breach notification requirement does require the cloud provider to inform its customer. And the customer may then be obliged to inform relevant state residents of the fact of the breach.

The US position is in fact very much more complex. The breach notification requirements of a US state apply to any company that holds data about a resident of that state even if that company does not operate in that state (nor use a cloud or other provider in that state). Accordingly, a UK company selling services into the US with its customers throughout the US may – in theory – have to look at the laws applicable in each of those states. In other words, there need be no relation with the US state in question other than the fact that the customer holds data about one of its residents, and the state's data breach law – in theory – then applies.

> **PRACTICAL TIP**
>
> If a customer's US-based cloud provider suffers a breach, and informs the customer (as it is obliged to do), the customer should consider whether or not to get local advice in relation to each of the various US states. US law is likely to require the customer to inform US residents in any case.

7.7   Key points

In this chapter we have explored what requirements might exist to notify individuals or regulators of security breaches in the cloud. Key points are as follows.

◆ The UK does not have a mandatory notification requirement generally applicable to all sectors. There will, however, as a result of recent amendments to the E-Privacy Directive [26], shortly be such a requirement imposed upon telecom companies and ISPs.

◆ The ICO has issued detailed guidance specifying the circumstances in which it thinks a notification should be voluntarily made to it by data controllers.

◆ The UK government and the NHS is operating such a regime on a 'voluntary' basis (imposed by the Prime Minister's office).

◆ A cloud customer in the UK using a provider in another country (in particular the US) might find that the laws of that other country apply to a data breach. US law generally requires the provider to inform the customer.

8 Software licensing and the cloud

8.1 Introduction

The software licensing issues that arise in cloud computing depend very much on what type of cloud services are being considered. A software as a service (SaaS) provision should not present too many difficulties (at least for the customer). In just the same way as a customer would license software in a traditional 'on-premises' acquisition, it obtains rights to use that software through the SaaS service. The provider ensures that it has any third party rights it needs to include.

However, when the service being considered is infrastructure as a service (IaaS), say, with a view to the customer transferring its existing software suite onto a virtualized infrastructure the situation can be complicated. Rights need to be cleared and contracts examined. In this chapter we explore these issues as well as open source issues on the cloud.

8.2 Moving existing licensing structures to the cloud

8.2.1 Introduction

In a nutshell the legal difficulty with moving an existing suite of software onto an IaaS service is that much of that software will have been licensed in from third parties on terms which did not necessarily anticipate a cloud service. It should be noted that this issue might arise not only when a third party IaaS provider is engaged but also when the move is onto a 'private cloud'.

Software licences vary significantly between providers, but one feature which is common across virtually all mainstream software houses is that the terms of use of the software are in some way restricted. It is these restrictions which present the problem; the move to the cloud may well take use of the software outside the scope of the licence and lead to the continuing use being both in breach of contract (of the software licence terms) and an infringement of intellectual property (as it will not have been authorized by the owner).

8.2.2 Restrictions to be considered

Table 2 sets out common software licence restrictions which may be relevant for consideration when moving software onto a cloud service.

Table 2. Common restrictions in software licences (possibly) preventing use in the cloud

Restriction	Cloud consequence
Software may be used only on a specified computer (or one of a particular specification) ...	That computer will no longer be used in the virtualized environment ...
... or at a specified location	... and not the cloud!
Software may only be used on one (but not specified) computer	The processing power of the application may be spread across a number of different 'virtual machines', or indeed even one 'virtual machine' which is spread across any number of physical machines.
Software may be used only by the licensee itself ...	The software owner might argue (whether successfully would depend on the actual language in the licence) that running the software in a cloud environment on a platform supplied by a third party involves use by that third party (albeit on the customer's behalf).
The software is confidential	Giving the software to a third party may well trigger a breach of confidentiality provisions (unless outsourcing – cloud or otherwise – was expressly envisaged).
Software is warranted and indemnified only against infringement of UK intellectual property (IP)	The cloud infrastructure may be outside the UK. If there are third party IP issues outside the UK, the contract now does not allow the consequences of that risk to be passed by the customer to the software house. Moreover, in some countries (notably, the US) it is easier for rights holders to obtain patents – and so in any case there is a greater IP risk in those countries than the UK.

The issues on legacy licences arise not only when putting systems into a public cloud IaaS system, but also when being put onto a private cloud or simply a virtualized service.

PRACTICAL TIP

Even if not bought with a view to installation in the cloud, software licences should always be carefully checked to ensure they permit use by a service provider on behalf of the licensee (whether cloud or traditional outsourcing).

8.2.3   The provider's risk

This is not simply an issue for the customer. A cloud provider hosting on its IaaS infrastructure software which has been put onto that infrastructure in breach of the customer's licence terms will itself potentially have liability. If it has possession of the software, it is likely to itself be doing acts which need the proprietor's permission. It will not have that permission and so will itself in this scenario be infringing the third party's rights. Whilst an indemnity can be used to pass the financial risk back onto the customer, it is nonetheless recommended that the provider also undertakes diligence as it may well find itself a bigger target than the customer. An indemnity is only as good as the financial worth of the customer.

PRACTICAL TIP

When moving an existing software suite onto an IaaS service, a customer should undertake an early investigation of the licensing position. Cloud providers should ask to see software licences, and will want to be indemnified in any case to protect themselves from the risk of a third party claim from a proprietor.

8.2.4   Evolution of new licensing models

Some software vendors are developing new licensing strategies designed to facilitate use on the cloud. Oracle has partnered with Amazon to allow its software (either under existing licences or new licences) to be used on the Amazon EC2 IaaS service. Clearly, the problems highlighted above should then not arise when a specific permission has been given for use on a cloud infrastructure. However, here, again, is a potential issue on vendor lock-in. If a package is acquired from a software house for use on a particular cloud platform (say, Amazon EC2), there is the obvious concern for the customer that the software licence does not permit use on any other IaaS if and when it wants to change provider.

8.3 Open source and the cloud

8.3.1 Introduction

Open source software (sometimes called free software) is software created by developers who subscribe to the belief that software which is open for anyone to fix and improve is inherently more stable. As such, and in marked contrast to the proprietary software industry, the source codes of the software are generally published and made available to anyone. Copyright still subsists in that software, but the owner of the copyright will generally license it on one of an ever-growing number of standard software terms, the most well known of which are those published by the Free Software Foundation (including the GNU[44] General Public License (GPL), which comes in a number of versions).

It is a common feature of these licences to require that when the licensed open source software is further distributed by a licensee, the source codes of that software must also be made available to the licensee's users. Some licences go further and say that when the open source software is 'built into' a bigger piece of software, the source codes of the whole of that bigger piece of software must also be made available to users; this is the so-called viral effect (as the open nature of the software 'infects' other software) or the 'copyleft' principle, and we explore this in the cloud context further on.

However, before doing so it is worth pointing out that there is another way in which open source arises in the cloud computing field. Open source software might be used as an infrastructure or development tool by the provider. Much of the software which is being used by providers of cloud services has been developed and licensed in accordance with open source principles. There are already prominent examples of this in relation to such software as virtualization software, file storage software, and other software at the infrastructure level. Except to the extent that, say, use of infrastructure software as part of a service which is then sold onto users might properly be classified as 'distribution' leading to the copyleft problem (as described further on), there are in fact no novel legal issues arising

---

[44] The name of a particular piece of open source software published by the Freedom Software Foundation, the GNU operating system; 'GNU' is a recursive acronym for 'GNU's not Unix'.

simply because the applications which might be developed are built using open source components or tools. All that the provider needs to do is the normal step of ensuring that its intended use is within the scope of the terms of the licence.

8.3.2   *Provision of software to a SaaS customer – the copyleft problem*

Open source software might be a component of software which is then provided as a service to a cloud customer. This raises the issue of whether the larger work incorporating the open source component itself becomes subject to the terms upon which the original open source software is licensed. Such terms could include an obligation on the licensee that it must distribute the program in source code as well as compiled form. In other words, whether it is infected as a result of a viral, copyleft provision.

Each of the many different types of open source licences deals with this issue in its own different way, and it is important for any software developer or reseller to examine carefully the terms of any open source software component it wants to use, in particular to determine whether any new software (or revision to the open source component) would in turn be subject to the original open source licence terms. For example, one of the most popular open source licences, the GNU General Public License (v 2.0), requires that a licensee that modifies and creates a 'work based on the program' must also distribute the source code of not only the original open source software, but also of the 'work based on the program' – the viral effect. The Lesser General Public License ('LGPL'), which is designed for the license of open source libraries, tries to draw a distinction (not too clear to apply in practice) between a work 'based on' the library and a work 'that uses' the library. The former contains code derived from the library, whereas the latter must be combined with the library in order to run. It is only the former which in theory is subject to the viral effect; source codes of a work 'based on' the library must be distributed if the work itself is distributed. However, there is a trap for the unwary: if the new work is linked to the library before distribution (which it may be if a fully built executable is distributed) then that is not a work 'that uses' the library; it is instead a work 'based on' the library (because it then contains portions of the library).

PRACTICAL TIP

In any environment (even non-cloud), use of open source components in a proprietary software solution which is then made available to customers needs care. There might (depending on the terms used and what is done with the software) be an accidental requirement to make source code of the new software generally available.

8.3.3   The viral effect in the cloud – the Affero Licences

The rationale of the free source movement including a 'viral' component is of course to free up all code; if a provider is to distribute the derived work, then the source codes should also be distributed. What the earlier versions of these licences assumed however was that there would be a 'distribution': a physical dissemination of the software into the actual possession of the users. When the software is made available to users as a service, there is (at least arguably) no distribution of the software. After all, the software never leaves the server of the provider.

As a result, new open source licences have emerged designed to fix this loophole, notably the Affero Licences. There are in fact two such licences under very similar names. The original 'Affero GPL', which was initially published by Affero Inc in 2002, was based on the GNU GPL v 2.0. It was designed to deal with SaaS issues (although in those days of course, SaaS was not the term used – instead the term used was application service provision). GNU has itself now published a successor to that based on the GNU GPL v 3.0, and known as the 'GNU Affero GPL'.

There is no express mention in either version of software as a service or indeed even application service provision. (The Free Software Foundation has been very critical of both the concept of 'cloud computing'[45] and the use of the term which they consider to be 'a marketing buzzword with no clear meaning'.)[46] Instead, the licences focus on users interacting with (not 'using') the software through servers. Specifically, the GNU Affero GPL (clause 13) states that the source code of any modified version must be available to users of the software when the software is offered to 'users interacting with it remotely through a computer network', which is clearly wide enough to cover use through a cloud service. The source codes have to be provided from the server 'through some standard or customary means of facilitating copying of software', and of course at no charge.

Software which is within this viral effect is the original software or any work which is a 'modified' version of the software (or, another expression used, a work 'based on' the earlier work). (The GNU Affero licence here uses terminology which was present in the GNU GPL licences.)

One difficulty with the GNU licences is that the concept of what is a 'modified version' is unclear. The GNU website says simply: 'Where's the line between two separate programs, and one program with two parts? This is a legal question, which ultimately judges will decide.' Its own preferred view is to focus on the means of communication between the two parts. If the two parts are bound together in the same executable, then the whole is a 'modified' version of the original. This is

---

[45]   See reference to Richard Stallman's comments in 1.2.
[46]   http://www.gnu.org/philosophy/words-to-avoid.html

so, says the FSF, even if in terms of quantity of lines of code or even in terms of relative importance of functionality, the original is a relatively minor part.

It is clear that great care is needed.

8.4 Software escrow in the cloud

8.4.1 Escrow in a traditional environment

In a traditional 'on-premises' licence the software house does not readily give a customer access to source codes.[47] The customer is therefore reliant on the software house (or a contractual support partner) for ongoing support such as bug fixes and functionality improvements. Software escrow is a mechanism used to enable the customer to get hold of the source codes (necessary for correcting and improving the software) in the event of a failure by the provider itself to support the software, either because it is in breach of the support contract or because it is insolvent. The source codes are put in the hands of an 'escrow agent', a third party (for example, NCC Escrow, Iron Mountain or Intellect) who enters into a tri-partite agreement with both the customer and the software house setting out the circumstances ('trigger events') under which the agent is obliged to provide the customer with the source codes. The following are the normal trigger events.

a) Software house insolvency – this could lead to automatic release of the source codes as there can be no argument as to whether it has occurred or not (at least in the case of formal insolvency proceedings such as an appointment of an administrator or liquidator).

b) Software house default – a typical software escrow agreement would provide for release on the breach (perhaps material breach) by the software house of particular provisions (normally the obligation to correct an error). The release is not automatic as it is not always clear that there has been a default. The

---

[47] The human readable element in which the software is written, a valuable trade secret of most software houses. Source codes are turned into machine-readable executables by a process called compilation.

licensee would notify the escrow agent of an alleged breach. The licensor is informed and, if it disagrees, a dispute resolution process is instigated with the escrow agent as the adjudicator to determine whether (as the customer says) the software house has in fact breached the relevant provision in the relevant way. If so, source codes are released.

8.4.2   Escrow in a SaaS environment

Traditional escrow does not work in a SaaS environment. The customer does not even have a copy of the executable in the first place. If there is a supplier insolvency, it is not only an issue of loss of support, there is the more fundamental risk of losing the application itself as well as the loss of data. Nonetheless, escrow agents have identified a solution intended even to guard against this risk. New services are coming into the market under which the SaaS provider is obliged to deposit with the escrow agent not only source codes but also the executable program and customer data. The intention is that on the SaaS solution being unavailable the customer can – in theory – run the application on an alternative infrastructure. As many SaaS vendors are operating on fairly standard IaaS or PaaS infrastructures provided by Amazon, Google and other big players, this may not be as far fetched as it sounds. (Clearly, given the early stages of this service, experience is limited, and it remains to be seen whether there is much take-up of these services.)

As with traditional escrow it is important that the deposit is actually verified – it is too late to find out in the event of a SaaS provider's failure that a critical component of software was not deposited.

PRACTICAL TIP

If relying on software escrow as a protective measure, a customer should consider utilizing the escrow agent's 'verification' service to ensure that what is in fact deposited is what should have been deposited, that is, that the deposited materials can recreate the actual service used.

As mentioned, the executable and the source codes are not enough; data needs also to be safeguarded – and that is within some escrow provider's cloud solutions. As the data will constantly be changing, there should be obligations to deposit data on a regular basis. Care is needed here as some of the standard offerings in this space state that the provider is to make a deposit of applications and data only every three months. This is likely to be inadequate for almost all commercial uses. Of course depending on the nature of the data being held in the cloud even a daily deposit might not be adequate, and what is needed is a real-time data replication service. These services too are being offered by agents. Clearly all this is an additional cost which needs to be borne in mind when undertaking the cost of ownership analysis of whether to go into the cloud in the first place.

> **PRACTICAL TIP**
>
> To be useful in a SaaS environment, software escrow needs also to deal with deposits of data (or at least the customer needs continuous alternative access to current data).

Any escrow arrangement for a SaaS solution would require the usual trigger events of supplier breach of support or insolvency for release of the deposited materials. However, it might also be useful to include a critical failure of relevant service levels (too much service interruption and downtime).

8.5 Key points

In this chapter we have explored software licensing issues arising in the cloud. Key points are as follows.

♦ A customer wishing to run an existing system on a cloud infrastructure should ensure that its software licences permit the transportation. Existing software will have been licensed on documentation that may not have envisaged use in a cloud environment and may contain any of a wide variety of restrictions which may catch the situation.

♦ A breach of such a restriction will put the customer in breach of contract and both the customer and the provider in a situation of infringing the third-party software house's intellectual property rights. A provider will want to be indemnified.

♦ Open source licences sometimes have a 'viral' ('copyleft') effect when the software is distributed to the public; the software company that uses the open source component may also have to make source code of its own software available to the wider public. Whilst older forms of open source licences were doubtful as to whether a SaaS distribution triggered this obligation, the newer form of 'Affero' licences puts the matter beyond doubt if the new software is a 'modified' version of the original software. Great care is needed when using open source components in building a SaaS offering.

♦ Software escrow solutions are difficult to apply in the cloud, but the escrow industry is beginning to develop products that could be considered. They may need to deal with data in a dynamic fashion and be relatively 'open' in allowing transfer to other infrastructures with ease. Escrow solutions should always be 'verified'.

9 Customer data: the provider's use of data, access to data and lock-in

9.1 Introduction

In this chapter we deal with a number of issues concerning customer data. A cloud provider has possession of the customer's data and is possibly the only person to possess it. One fundamental issue to be dealt with in a cloud contract therefore is the ability of the customer to regain possession of the data on termination. Particularly pertinent here are considerations around obtaining data when the provider is insolvent.

We begin though with another issue which can be contentious.

9.2 The provider's use of its customer's data

Another area of possible contention and mismatch between a customer and provider is the issue of use by a provider of the customer's data. A cloud provider may want to reserve a right itself to use the customer's data for some purpose other than providing services to the customer. A cloud provider (especially of a SaaS variety) will be sitting on an immense quantity of its customers' data which, when aggregated together, can be of immense value – it can be analysed for example to create a report based on that data. For example, the US payroll provider ADP creates its ADP Employment Report – a report on private employment in the United States derived from aggregated and anonymous ADP payroll data from 500,000 of its customers.

Another example would be a SaaS solution which administers customer transactions on their behalf. The cloud provider would be able to analyse relevant data and then provide a report on the typical transactions that are happening in that field either to its customers generally, to those customers that are willing to pay for this enhanced service, or to the public generally. The idea would be that each customer (or subscribing customer) benefits from the report and the market knowledge gleaned from the general customer base. A report could be issued say on the typical commercial terms of particular trades (market prices, average quantities, nature of transactions, etc.). A provider will naturally give an assurance that data in the report will not identify a particular customer.

A customer will often be reluctant to allow any such use. It may have a number of objections. First, it may fear the security risks. Any customer that had been at pains to ensure security policies were properly present will very understandably feel that any use by the provider other than the provision of a basic 'vanilla' service will increase the risk of something going wrong with the security (and at worst a breach leading to data leakage). Secondly, and related to the first reason, despite any assurance that the provider may give in relation to anonymization of the data, there will be a fear that somehow different pieces of data which might be anonymous on their own could be put together to identify the customer. In other words, certainly for larger customers, the reports may be capable of being reverse-engineered to reveal underlying individual data points. Thirdly, a customer may be disgruntled that the provider is able to make money out of the customer's data: surely, the customer may think, it should be paid for? The provider will of course say that it too will benefit from the report or added value the data allows it to provide and that that is payment enough (assuming that the report is part of the service actually subscribed for). This brings us to the fourth and last reason for the customer's reluctance. A customer will not want its data to benefit its competitors even if its competitors' data benefits it. This is especially true of large users who may well be 'setting the trend' in the market and therefore fear that any such report will not add to what it already knows about the market. Smaller customers may not have that concern.

PRACTICAL TIP

Contracts should be carefully scrutinized by the customer to ensure that it fully understands the limitations on use of data which the provider is volunteering. If there are none expressly dealing with the issue, then one should be suggested.

Some cloud providers faced with strong objections from their customers have now dropped permissive language which previously appeared in their contracts. Other providers still include language allowing them to do this and attempt to allay customers' fears by giving some explanation as to what they are doing. It is clear, that any clause as stark as 'SaaS provider can use the customer's data for generating reports or providing value added services' will find understandable objection.

PRACTICAL TIP

If a provider is keen to provide any additional service which depends on the customer's data then it should expect concern from its customers. A provider should avoid 'stark' clauses retaining the right to use the data for indefinite or very wide purposes. Examples of how the data will be used, which focus on the value to the customer of the resulting reports, are likely to be more palatable.

Cloud providers should consider expanding on this in FAQs.

9.3   Access to data on exit

9.3.1   Provider lock-in

A cloud provider has possession of the customer's data and possibly is the only person with that possession. One fundamental issue to be dealt with in a cloud contract therefore is the ability of the customer to regain possession on termination. A customer's concern as to whether or not it can actually do so (or do so economically) is one of the main reasons for customer reluctance to move data into the cloud.[48]

It is difficult to overstate the risks here. In the modern world many businesses' life-blood is its data and a fear of loss of control of that data is a major issue that customers venturing into the cloud for the first time will have to overcome. There are a couple of related issues. First, how does the customer get the data back, if at all? Secondly, is the data going to be in a format which the customer can use? A customer will not want the data in a proprietary format as that would 'lock-in' the customer to a particular provider. These issues raise a number of overlapping issues: commercial, technical and legal.

PRACTICAL TIP

It is essential in any adoption of cloud that the customer knows commercially, technically and legally how it will get access to data at all times.

---

[48]   Richard Stallman's view (that cloud computing is 'stupidity' for just this reason) was noted in 1.2.

9.3.2 *Commercial issues*

Taking the commercial issues first. A customer will often want to ensure that it has an entitlement to download the data at any time of its choosing or at least to be provided with a copy of the data on a regular basis. It is not sufficient only to have an obligation upon the provider to deliver a copy of the data, as that is something which may well be very difficult to enforce for two main reasons. First, the relationship may not at the time of exit be particularly amicable. This could be because the termination is through an allegation of breach (by either the customer or the provider against the other). It may be because the customer simply wants to move away from the particular solution with an inevitable disappointment for the provider of a loss of a potentially lucrative revenue stream. Secondly, the provider could be insolvent and may immediately cease trading. A contractual obligation will be of little use as there might be immediate staff losses and no one to assist in an orderly exit. Even if there is not an immediate cessation of business (say where an administrator is appointed to try and save a going concern), the priority for staff and management (who might be under threat of job losses themselves) will be to do what they can to win new business, cut costs, and look after those customers who are not terminating. A customer that is terminating might expect little assistance in practice even when there is a contractual entitlement.

For these reasons, a customer should not want to leave it until a termination event to test its ability to obtain the data. It may be that a feature of the service simply allows the customer the ability to download the data at any time and without recourse to the provider, and if so there seems little that can go wrong (other than the servers ceasing operation on termination). It will be prudent for the customer to ensure that the functionality does work and to do so on a regular basis (with a full download), and that it is possible to receive the data in the correct format. For particular services, it might be advisable for the customer to take a back-up of data on a regular basis itself. Escrow services which cover data might also be useful in this regard (as to which see 8.4.2). In short, the customer should ensure that it does not wholly rely on the provider for the data or at least should be fully aware of the risks of doing so. Of course, any alternative data storage/duplication solution will have a cost and effort which might detract from some of the cost-savings and efficiency benefits of the cloud proposition.

PRACTICAL TIP

Customers should ensure that they have ready access to data on an ongoing basis. They need to carefully consider whether the risk of having only one copy of their data with one cloud provider is a risk that they are willing to take.

9.3.3   Technical issues

Data is of course always stored in a particular format and a customer will not wish to simply trust the provider to return data in a format of the customer's choice. The data might then arrive in a proprietary format of the provider which will not easily enable the customer to migrate to an alternative solution. This is a problem that also exists in traditional outsourcing or bureau servicing arrangements. In those cases the parties might rely on a provision providing for the customer (at the time of exit) to determine the format of the data, perhaps providing for data to be supplied in a 'reasonably appropriate' format or something similar specified by the customer. An outsourcing provider will insist on charging for the conversion. Whilst this can of course also work in a cloud environment, it does detract from a central aspect of the cloud model; namely, that the offering should be standard given the multi-tenancy architecture. The provider at the exit stage could supply a tool for conversion into the customer-specified format, which the customer can then itself use to migrate. Again, the provider will want to charge for this, and again, there is a detraction from the cost benefit. Having said that, there is an argument that as tools for migration from the provider's format to one of its competitor's format is something which would be used time and again it should not be a cost that an individual customer should bear.

A solution that does not permit the provider to charge additional sums would need to be specific about the type of format. At the time of signing the contract the customer will obviously not know what technology it will be moving to following termination. (And of course, even if it did, it would be back to the situation of a tailored offering departing from the standard offering.) The contract could specify a fairly standard non-proprietary format, which will clearly have the attraction for the provider of being consistent across all customers. Some providers, for example, specify that data will be returned in the ubiquitous 'comma-separated values' (CSV) format (which is supported by many database-based applications). After all, any replacement provider should be able to import data from a standard non-proprietary format.

PRACTICAL TIP

Customers will want contracts to be specific in relation to the format in which the data will be returned.

9.3.4   Legal issues

Once the commercial and technical issues are addressed, the legal issues will largely fall into place. The contract needs to reflect the negotiated position on those issues. However, in an insolvency situation the contract may simply not work.

As noted, in practice, a company which may be desperately trying to survive is more likely to give full attention to revenue generating matters (such as keeping continuing customers happy and ongoing sales effort), rather than assisting those customers who are terminating (even if those customers have a binding contractual right). To safeguard against the possibility that the provider will not give up the data, the customer may well want a right to enter premises and obtain the data itself. Of course, as is the position with audit rights mentioned previously,[49] this is only likely to be relevant or cost-effective to enforce when, first, the customer knows where the data is and, secondly, it is in the same jurisdiction. Even if such a right is ignored by the provider, in an extreme situation an emergency court order might be attainable.

There is an additional point. It shouldn't be assumed that, following termination of the contract, the provider will always delete the customer's data. A customer that wishes to ensure that after termination the provider no longer has a copy of the data in its possession should also ensure that there is an express obligation in the agreement dealing with the point (but only after a copy has been provided to the customer).

> **PRACTICAL TIP**
>
> Ownership of data by a customer does not necessarily imply that a provider is obliged to return that data to the customer. There must always be an express contractual obligation upon the provider to return (or at least make available) the data to the customer.
>
> There could also be an express obligation for the provider to delete all remaining copies once that has been done, perhaps after some post-termination period to ensure that there is sufficient time to retrieve a copy.

9.3.5 Contractual chains of cloud providers

The risks of a provider's insolvency or breach as it relates to the customer having reliable access to its own data is compounded when the data is not actually in the hands of the provider but instead in the hands of one of its subcontractors.

The SaaS space is full of small(ish) companies entering into the market by building their offerings on one of the principal PaaS offerings. Large SaaS providers also use outsourced hosting services. Whilst the data may well be safely secured behind state of the art security deployed by the PaaS provider (or its subcontractor) or the hosting company, it is at the SaaS level where the real risk is. The issue is compounded if there are more than two providers in the chain (see Figure 3 for an illustration).

---

[49] See 3.7.2.

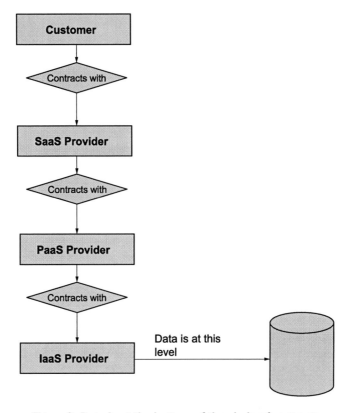

Figure 3. Data is at the bottom of the chain of contracts

If the SaaS provider is insolvent, whilst the data may well be very safe indeed, it is in the hands of a PaaS (or IaaS) provider (or, worst, one of its subcontractors). The customer will have real difficulty in retrieving the data from anyone lower down the chain. In the first place, the customer may simply not know where the data is (although this does of course depend on the extent of its diligence). Even when the customer does know where the data is, the PaaS or IaaS provider may simply not be interested in assisting the customer (who was not *its* customer). Certainly, the provider would want to be paid for any help. It may already be out of pocket given the fact that their direct customer (the provider above it in the chain) is insolvent.

However, even with the best will in the world the PaaS provider (the subcontractor of the insolvent SaaS provider) may not in practice be able to assist. The SaaS provider's data ultimately belongs to many customers, and one customer approaching the subcontractor for data will necessitate the identification of that data amongst many. It may simply not be possible to do so. The SaaS provider may only have been acquiring infrastructure space and any data may – in the hands of the PaaS provider – be encrypted or, even if not, may be simply 'raw' (without any formatting). In any case the data will be physically intermingled even if it is logically segregated. The PaaS provider may not be able to determine what data is what and which data is which customer's. As such, any approach to a provider further down the contractual chain is likely to be fraught with difficulties. (As mentioned elsewhere in this section, a customer needs to consider very carefully the risk of having all its data in one basket, as it were.)

PRACTICAL TIP

When contracting with a cloud provider, customers should understand (i) who, in fact, has the data, and (ii) the financial stability of the provider. New entrants to the market require specially careful scrutiny.

9.3.6 Lock-out and Coghead

An acknowledged fear for customers entering the cloud is the possibility of lock-in: the difficulty of a customer moving away from a particular cloud provider due either to the cost involved in moving data from one provider to another or the technical difficulties of doing so. The reverse is possible, as the Coghead situation demonstrated in 2009, it is possible to be 'locked-out' of a platform.

Coghead was a Californian company which offered a PaaS service allowing the building and hosting of custom online database applications. Applications were built around custom data collections and typically designed to facilitate the management of, and collaboration on, business data. The product was intended to allow users to design a range of applications from scratch using only a drag and drop, a What-You-See-Is-What-You-Get user interface, with very limited scripting or coding (if any) required. Coghead tried to attract 'tech-savvy business people' by limiting the amount of programming or design experience required to author applications in its platform. In February 2009, Coghead announced that it would be shutting down 'due to the impact of economic challenges'. It sold its intellectual property, including the Coghead service, to SAP for SAP to use as an internal resource. SAP imposed a lock-out from 30 April 2009 meaning that each Coghead customer had only 8 weeks to completely rewrite all their applications on an entirely new platform to prevent themselves from being in breach of contract to their own customers.

9.4 Key points

In this chapter we have explored customer data issues including use by the provider and lock-in. Key points are as follows.

- Some cloud providers wish to use customer data for purposes not directly related to the service being acquired by the customer. An example of this is aggregation into reports to report on the market generally (types and values of transactions, for example). This may not be objectionable to customers, but the leeway (if any) enjoyed by the provider should be carefully considered by the customer and set out expressly in the contract.

- It is imperative that there are no commercial, technical or legal obstacles to retrieval of the data by the customer. Lock-in can only be avoided where data is readily accessible in a useable format.

- Contracts should contain express obligations dealing with return of data to the customer on termination as well as obligations for the provider to delete all remaining copies.

- In practice, legal entitlements to access may not offer too much comfort when the provider is insolvent, especially when data is in fact in the possession of the provider's subcontractor. For this reason, customers should always consider ensuring they have access to alternative copies of the data.

10 Service definition – the provider's ability to change the service

10.1 Introduction

Typically cloud solutions are not tailored to specific customers. Each individual customer is acquiring a common solution used by all the providers' customers. The solution will therefore necessarily evolve as the provider seeks to continually improve the product and match market needs. The issue addressed in this chapter is the freedom the provider reserves in its contracts to change that solution, which will necessarily impact upon all customers. Once a customer has acquired the solution it is of course unrealistic to suppose that the service will not change. Indeed, a customer will want further improvements, both in functionality and in performance. Against that, however, the customer will not want changes that are so dramatic they require retraining of its personnel, nor changes that impact upon other systems which depend on the solution or interact with it. Moreover, the customer may well have acquired the solution on the basis of a particular feature and will not want that feature to be one that is 'improved' away from what it originally found attractive. There is a tension here which needs to be addressed.

10.2 A comparison with software licensing

Before proceeding to examine this tension in the cloud context, and to highlight the solutions that are beginning to emerge, it is worth considering the same issue as it arises in a more traditional 'on-premises' software acquisition. When software is licensed for installation on the customer's own infrastructure, the software installed is not typically different from that installed on the systems of any other customer. If a supplier issues a new version of the software (whether it is described as an 'upgrade', a new 'version', a 'release', a 'patch' or otherwise) the customer is not automatically forced to move onto the new version. Indeed, the superseded version can normally be used indefinitely, although support for it will naturally expire. A careful software licensee will normally try to ensure that there is a contractual commitment to support older versions of the package for a specified period of time (say, a number of years or months) or at least a restriction on there being 'too many' updates. This customer is trying to ensure that it does not have to go through the effort (and it can be a great deal of effort) of installing the upgrade. Apart from the fact that a software house does not want to maintain indefinitely a superseded version for any of its customers once any warranty has expired, it would not ordinarily care if the customer decided never to upgrade: primarily, it is the customer that loses out on new or corrected functionality and performance improvements.

Not all upgrade issues that are relevant to software licences are relevant in the cloud. For example, one of the customer's concerns is the desire to avoid having to upgrade its infrastructure (hardware or software). A new software release may require a newer version of an underlying database package or operating system or higher specification hardware, but this issue might not arise in the cloud when those items too are the responsibility of the provider.

10.3 From the provider's perspective

Like the software licensor operating under a traditional 'on premises' model, the cloud provider will constantly want to evolve its offering in order to remain competitive. It will want to keep abreast of its competition and their developments. It will want to deal with and hopefully anticipate its typical customer's concerns and desires. Generally, it wants to continually improve the product and to innovate. Where the comparison breaks down, however, is that, in on premises licensing, innovating the product does not (as just seen) automatically force existing customers to move onto the improved version. In the cloud, certainly where there is multi-tenancy, once a new version is introduced, all customers on that version will likely have to move onto the new version.

The cloud provider therefore wants complete flexibility. It must, in the end, be able to force the customer to upgrade. It has no real choice, the economics of the cloud model are predicated on the fact that all customers run on the same version of the software and perhaps in the same, multi-tenanted 'instance'.

> **PRACTICAL TIP**
>
> A provider should in its terms of business reserve the right to make changes to the services.

10.4 From the customer's perspective

The customer has been sold the proposition on the basis of its current functionality, which to get to the stage of negotiating contracts it must have found attractive. Nonetheless, no matter how attractive, especially in early adoptions, it might have had quite a lot of initial anti-cloud reluctance to overcome. The customer will have had a number of fears, including security and the lack of direct control over an important part of its IT offering. To then be presented with a contract which expressly gives the provider wide discretion to change that offering without reference to it may well make the customer pause. Yes, a customer may say to the provider, you are selling us an exciting and cost-effective package, but how do we know that that is what you will be providing in a few months time? After all, in an 'on-premises' software acquisition, the customer had the ability to decline or not install a new version of the software.

A customer may also fear that the removal of an element of functionality from the service is only a precursor to that element then finding its way into an additional option or plug-in for which there will be an additional charge.

PRACTICAL TIP

A customer should be wary of a completely unfettered ability for the provider to change the service, at least when the customer is tied into a long-term contract without a right to terminate early.

10.5   How to deal with service change in a cloud contract

Cloud contracts will not always be negotiable and often a customer has no power at all to insist upon a change to terms (certainly, when it is a small customer dealing with a giant provider). The following points assume that there is scope for some negotiation. In any case, providers hoping to avoid unsettling their customers when the latter are presented with a standard contract may wish to take a reasonable and measured stance on this issue. A customer will understandably resist a completely unfettered ability for the provider to change the offering. Whilst a first version of a cloud contract might include such an ability, a compromise is likely to better reflect a customer's concerns. Compromises will inevitably focus on different types of service changes. Nonetheless, given the multi-tenancy model, and cloud economics generally, the fetter on the provider's ability to change the service is likely to focus on the length of notice and not a giving up of the ability to make such changes.

First, a contract will have to deal with trivial changes. These are likely to be permitted by the contract (and without the requirement of any particular notice). An example would be service changes that have no impact on the functionality or the service levels.

Secondly, if the change is material or there is otherwise an impact upon the customer, then the customer will want to require notice to be given. Changes in this category would include those where a customer would have to spend money or effort (for example, upgrading its own systems) or even just change its processes (including the requirement for additional training). The actual period of notice is obviously subject to negotiation. It should be sufficiently long to allow the customer to make an informed decision as to what needs to be done and (if unhappy about the change or impact) ultimately to move to another supplier.

Thirdly, the provider might be required to make a change as a result of an intellectual property problem. The service may be found (or thought) to infringe the intellectual property rights of a third party. If a problem with intellectual property does occur then, in order to avoid infringing (and putting its customers also in danger), the provider will want to be able to immediately amend its offering to avoid the problem. This concept is capable of refinement. For example, the contract could stipulate that the provider can only make such changes if there is in fact a court order preventing the offering. A provider would never volunteer this; it would follow from a customer request. It would exacerbate the provider's potential liability in the interim to the third party. Accordingly, the contract might be more permissive and allow the change if the provider has a good faith or reasonable belief that there is a problem and that a court order would follow. Either way, a customer might seek to negotiate a right to terminate the agreement on any such change.

Similarly, a change might be permitted if the provider considers the change to be necessary to comply with a legal requirement. A provider may not volunteer notice for this type of change, but the customer will want no surprises and may take the view that, where it is something which the provider should have known about, notice should be given.

Lastly, a provider might also want to make changes without notice when it considers it necessary to do so for technical reasons or to ensure the continuing provision of the service without degradation or interruption. This is a little trickier for the customer to accept as – again – it is something which strictly the provider has in its control. It is reasonable for a customer to insist that the provider takes full responsibility for issues around its technical ability to provide the service. Nonetheless a provider may well want to guard against the unforeseen. A compromise on this point is to recognize that changes for such reasons might indeed come about unexpectedly and then to require that the provider gives the customer a period of notice if reasonably practicable, recognizing that it might not always be practical.

PRACTICAL TIP

Contracts could deal with change by making distinctions between different categories of changes: the more material the change, or the more necessitated for reasons within the provider's control, the longer the notice to be given to the customer.

A couple of additional points from the customer's perspective. First, the customer can take reassurance from, and should insist upon, a contractual provision which states that the changes will only be made in respect of the services it is acquiring if the same change is made in respect of all customers generally (and not just to it). Genuine 'technical reasons' or 'service enhancements', and so on, should be generally applicable. Secondly, in all these scenarios, whatever other safeguards are also present, a customer may want a right to terminate if it is dissatisfied with what remains of the offering following the change. A right to terminate, in a situation where the customer has paid in advance, may also be coupled with a right to receive a refund of monies paid for service which has not in fact been used. There is much scope for different solutions to this type of issue.

> **PRACTICAL TIP**
>
> In the event of certain types of service changes (certainly those that impact upon the customer's own internal processes or its retained IT), it might be appropriate for the customer to include a right to terminate in the contract.
>
> If the customer's protection is to terminate early, it should consider whether the contract should provide for a pro-rata refund of any monies paid in advance.

10.6 Key points

In this chapter we have explored service definition. Key points are as follows.

♦ Cloud economics imply that many customers will be using the same version of the service. Change mechanics have to recognize this; a cloud provider cannot permit any particular customer to have a say on whether or when changes are implemented.

♦ Nonetheless, a customer may resist a completely unfettered ability to change and the contract should deal with both parties' points of views. The customer will not want to be forced to accept changes that materially affect its enjoyment of the service (perhaps by the loss of functionality that it was accustomed to or by a need to retrain staff or to upgrade its own internal resources).

♦ It is only in exceptional circumstances (where a customized service is provided at a premium, for example) that a provider will agree to address the customer's concerns with some form of veto over its ability to enforce change. More normal, if anything is conceded at all, is a right for the customer to terminate early if it is unhappy with a change.

11 Service levels

11.1 Introduction

There are a number of trust issues which a prospective customer will have to overcome before venturing into the cloud. Security is foremost, of course, but so too is the issue of service availability and other quality issues. A customer needs to be able to trust that the solution (no longer in its direct control) will be available when it needs it. As well as being reliant on connectivity (internet or otherwise) to be able to access data, a customer also needs to rely on the provider maintaining its infrastructure, on which the cloud service is supplied, in a sufficiently robust manner. No service provider will give an absolute assurance that its service will be available 100% of the time (just as no software house would warrant that software is error free). Instead a typical cloud provider (if it offers anything at all) will offer some form of availability expressed as a percentage (typically in the range of 95% to 99.9%; rarely, higher). Cloud providers may well ask their customers, when considering the service level being offered, to compare the proposition with the customer's own existing service levels. Many customers will not even have measured availability when the service now being acquired externally was being managed internally.

The expression 'service level' is used to describe the ongoing promise of a provider to meet a particular standard in terms of availability, responsiveness, or other such measurable factors. In the cloud the most important service level will be availability, but there might be others. The service level system not only sets the target but frequently also sets the consequence of missing the target, often a system of service credits. This is a mechanic under which the customer is compensated by the provider if a promised level is not achieved. Service levels and credits sometimes appear in a separate document (or schedule) called a 'service level agreement' (SLA), which – despite its name – is not normally a separate contract in its own right; rather, it is part of the overall deal.

Some providers will publish their service level agreements on their websites and will not necessarily automatically provide a copy directly to a customer. These are important documents, and part of the overall deal, and should always be carefully reviewed.

A service level/credit regime has a few important and overlapping purposes. Its primary function is of course to set out the standard to which the service will be provided, an important part of the commercial and technical assessment that a customer must make in considering the offering. Then, it allows for compensation to the customer if that standard is not met. It also motivates the provider to meet that standard by providing for loss of revenue (through a service credit regime) if it does not meet promised levels.

Even the biggest cloud providers suffer outages. Rackspace, the internet hosting company, also provides cloud IaaS solutions from the same data centres. It has had a number of service outages including one in June 2009 sufficiently serious to merit a public statement (as they are a US listed company). They lost power to their data centre, but then the stand-by generators also failed. Customers were left without service for 40 min. As a result, Rackspace estimated in their statement that they would have to pay out service credits of as much as $3.5 million. Amazon had a major outage in 2008 that affected its S3 cloud network; this lasted for 7 to 8 hours. The best known of the SaaS providers, Salesforce.com, is not immune from service outages. In 2006, they suffered an outage which lasted 6 hours. In January 2009, they suffered a service disruption for about an hour due to a core network device failing. This is thought to have affected 900,000 users.

11.2 Typical service metrics

There are likely to be a number of metrics that make sense in any cloud context.

11.2.1 Availability

Each cloud offering (of whatever type) will require the provider to give a commitment that the service is actually 'available', and this is the most important measure and sometimes the only one which is in fact assured. Availability can be complex for a number of reasons, especially when the service might constitute a number of different elements. We explore this further in the subclauses that follow.

11.2.2 Service response times

Customers should consider whether to require a service response time level. This would measure the length of time needed for the service to perform a typical function, that is, from the request being placed until the service responds. A cloud user might for example be concerned that there are simply too many customers being serviced by the same (multi-tenancy) instance of the software. An assurance on response times would go some way to mitigating against this concern.

Such a service level is not often volunteered. If it does feature in an SLA, the cloud provider would certainly exclude the time taken for data to be communicated (as internet connectivity would not normally be in the provider's control).

11.2.3 Problem resolution times

There can be a variety of metrics around this issue. How long before a reported problem is logged and allocated a priority? How long before a work-around is issued? How long before a full solution is provided? (This is belt and braces as of course if a problem is not resolved, the availability measure might also be triggered. Nonetheless, it can be useful to have, especially as repeated failures to resolve problems in a particular timescale can be a warning sign of greater problems to come.)

11.2.4 Elasticity

One of the benefits for a cloud computing customer is the ability to scale quickly. It is possible to measure the speed at which an additional resource (servers, storage, and so on) is made available following a customer request, and for the provider to commit to a particular level. It might be worth the customer insisting upon such a service level if there is a frequent requirement for such flexibility.

11.3 Availability

The most important metric in a cloud offering is the assurance to the customer that the service is available, ideally 24/7, 365 days per year. Depending on the type of service there might be an agreed period of 'dead time', during which period scheduled maintenance might be performed – in exactly the same way as would be the case if the relevant service was being provided in-house by the customer's IT department.

Saying that a service will be 'available' a particular percentage of time, say 99.9%, raises a few issues of definition. What is meant by available? Is, say, a SaaS service designed for use by many hundreds of customer employees across the glove available if just one employee in the UK (or just the employees in the UK) can use the service?

PRACTICAL TIP

The contract needs to be very clear on what 'availability' means. Is the system available if one user (or one location) can use some (if not all functionality)? Is it 'unavailable' if only one user cannot access full functionality?

Then, over what period is availability measured? A promise of, say, 99.9% availability is ambiguous unless it can be tested and therefore the period over which the measurement is to be taken needs to be clearly set out. As may be obvious, and as will be illustrated below, there is a big difference in terms of potential disruption to a customer between 99.9% availability measured over a year than the same figure of 99.9% availability measured over a day. As much care is therefore needed around the definitions in an SLA as in any other part of the contract.

The gold standard SLA for availability are the 'five nines' of 99.999%, but that is fairly rare. To take a small and possibly non-representative sample of what the leading cloud providers publicly offer in terms of availability: Amazon EC2 is at 99.95%, Google App Engine and Microsoft Azure are both at 99.9%. These numbers can appear to be encouragingly high. However, it all depends on the period over which availability is measured. Table 3 further on shows how much downtime is allowed by such figures over various measuring periods. Whilst from an initial look there is not much difference between 99.99% availability and 99.0%, the former only allows just less than 1 hour downtime over a year, whilst the latter allows over 3.5 days a year. Moreover, if something like 99.9% is acceptable in principle, an SLA providing for measurement over a year allows a downtime of 8 hours 45 min over the year and it needs to be borne in mind that all 8 hours 45 min could occur on the same day. If the service was down for 8 hours (even during the peak period), there would be no service level failure. Contrast this with the other extreme: if 99.9% is measured daily, a service level failure would occur if only 1 min's or so disruption occurred on a particular day.

PRACTICAL TIP

Customers should pay particular attention to the period over which a given service level is measured.

Sometimes availability is not measured in respect of the entire day, but only some form of (perhaps, extended) working day. This may of course be fine, but again simple arithmetic shows drafting issues which a customer should bear in mind. If the service is one where a customer expects realistically to use it only during the working day, a customer will want to look closely at the time over which the availability is assured (to the appropriate level). For example, 99% availability allows 14 min over a 24 hour period (but all of those 14 min might be in the, say, 12 hour working day). By contrast, 99% availability assured over a 12 hour working day allows 7 min during that period. Because of this, some providers do draw a distinction between availability during core period and during non-core (slow) periods.

Table 3. Permitted downtime by the 9s

	Annual	Monthly	Daily (24 hours)
99.999%	5.259 min	0.438 min	0.0144 min
99.99%	52.59 min	4.38 min	0.144 min
99.9%	8 h 45.6 min	43.8 min	1.4 min
99%	3 days 15 hours	7 hours 18 min	14.4 min

11.4   The consequences of missing service levels

11.4.1   Target or contractual level?

The precise consequence of missing any level depends on the particular contract. The usual remedy is a credit on missing the service level. However, some SLAs include two figures in respect of a particular service level: one a target and the other a lower figure to indicate failure. A remedy is then only offered for failing to meet the lower level. From a provider's point of view, it sets a target which it aspires to and allows the provider to genuinely boast about a higher level in their sales literature. From the customer's point of view, such a promise could be seen as verging on the disingenuous as, most likely, the customer has no remedy at all unless the lower figure is missed. Customers should therefore take care.

> **PRACTICAL TIP**
>
> Depending on precise drafting, a 'target' level (as the name suggests) is aspirational only; there will likely be no contractual consequence if that level is not met.

11.4.2   Credits and other remedies

The normal mechanism used in an SLA to compensate the customer for receiving a sub-standard service is for the customer to earn service credits. These are normally monetary discounts from either past or future invoices. A typical service credit may state that for each minute or hour or x% non-availability below the trigger level, the cloud customer will receive a credit in a specified amount. The specified amount might be a day's fees or pro-rata reflecting the period of non-availability. If it is at too low a level, it will not really be a carrot incentivizing the provider.

PRACTICAL TIP

A customer needs to ensure that the level of credit is meaningful to ensure its purposes: compensating it for loss of service and properly incentivizing the provider.

A customer should also note carefully the contractual language. This is not a refund of fees paid, only a credit against future invoices. (If this is towards the end of the agreement, there may be no future invoice.)

Whilst credits are the normal remedy, some providers (notably, Google App Engine) instead offer additional free service (i.e. an extension of the term) for failure. Clearly, this is less attractive to a customer: it is unhappy with the service and all it gets as compensation for that unhappiness is additional service.

11.4.3 Calculating credits

There are mechanics around a typical service credit regime that merit appropriate scrutiny by the customer. These often detract from the initially anticipated benefit of the regime in a less than obvious manner. First, there will inevitably be caps on the amount of credit that can be earned. The total that might be earned for service failure could be as low as 10% of the recurring fees for the service (whether the monthly, quarterly or annual fee). In effect, this causes pain to the provider by severely reducing its profit or eliminating it altogether but not so much pain as to actually put the particular account into a loss. Caps, however, may be more complicated than simply one overall cap. Each of a number of different service levels offered by the provider might have a separate credit regime, and in relation to each such regime, there might be a cap at a particular percentage of the fees for that regime.

PRACTICAL TIP

A service level or credit regime should be considered as a whole, and the cap on any credit is an important part of that whole. Customers should be wary about it being set too low.

The effect of a cap can be far reaching. Once the service misses the target by a particular amount or on a number of occasions during the period, the cap will be reached. The purpose of incentivizing the provider to fix problems quickly will be removed; having reached the cap, there is no longer this incentive to fix the underlying problem as the provider cannot lose any more money by having to pay increased credits. (That is not to say there are no other incentives – clearly, any reputable provider will want to limit damage to its goodwill that any prolonged outage would entail.)

11.4.4 Exhaustive remedy

It is standard for the provider to include in its contract a clause stating that the service credit regime is the exhaustive or exclusive remedy for failure to provide the service. In other words, if the service is unavailable, all the customer can do is recover credits – it cannot also seek to claim more general 'damages', e.g. loss of revenues that would have been made had the service been available. A customer could try and resist such a provision, especially if there is also a cap at a fairly low level on the credits.

11.5 Standard exceptions

Cloud providers in common with other IT and telecom service providers that commit to a (more or less) continuous availability of a resource to the customer often include a number of fairly standard exceptions to the service level commitment. In this section we set out those that are common.

11.5.1 Force majeure

English contract law is very strict. Other than when a contract becomes literally impossible to perform as stipulated, a party is bound to perform no matter how difficult (or costly) it is to actually do so. So if there is a fire or flood at a data centre, say, the provider is not normally excused performance as it is of course possible for the provider to commission an alternative centre; English law would disregard the costs of doing so in forcing the provider to perform. Of course. it is open for the parties to agree that the provider should be released from its obligation if that sort of unexpected event were to arise. 'Force majeure' is an expression which is used to encapsulate those types of events and a clause frequently appears in contracts excusing the provider both from primary obligations under the contract as well as commitments to provide the services to a specified level should such an event occur.

In an SLA context, a typical clause would state that the service level should not apply during a period when the force majeure event was in existence and preventing a particular level being met. Further, the force majeure concept is sometimes extended to allow an excuse when the force majeure event occurs not only to the provider itself but also to the provider's suppliers. In the cloud context this is likely to be particularly relevant. The SaaS provider, for example, who contracts with an IaaS or PaaS provider for infrastructure or platform, will want to rely on this provision if a fire was to occur at the latter's data centre and so on.

Care is needed in considering what events fall within the exception. A provider will want as many as possible (within reason). The following would usually feature (and should not be too problematic to a customer in a sense that they are standard):

a) acts of God, war, riot, civil commotion;

b) accident, fire, flood or storm;

c) strikes and other employee disputes;

d) a 'catch all' of events beyond the control (sometimes, the wider: beyond the 'reasonable' control) of the party.

The following may also sometimes appear and a customer may well find these more objectionable:

- failure of hardware: a customer would expect the provider to ensure proper maintenance;

- disruption of power supply: a provider might be expected to ensure it has stand-by generators and take responsibility if those fail (see the description of Rackspace's outage mentioned at 11.1);

- communications problem: this is perhaps unacceptable when it is wide enough to cover links between, say, different aspects of the providers infrastructure, as opposed to the internet generally;

- failures caused by other customers: this could be resisted by a customer on the grounds that it is up to the provider to ensure that its shared systems are sufficiently robust to withstand any use (including misuse) by its customers;

- default of one of its suppliers. This is dealt with in detail in the next section.

PRACTICAL TIP

Force majeure clauses are sometimes treated as standard 'boilerplate' (and indeed often appear under the 'Miscellaneous' heading at the end of contracts). However, they contain important and sometimes surprising exceptions to the supplier's obligation to provide the services. They must always be carefully reviewed.

11.5.2   Third-party suppliers

Somewhat related to force majeure, and indeed sometimes dealt with within that clause itself, is an exception which allows the provider to avoid liability if a failure is due to its suppliers. There are two separate issues here.

First, when a force majeure event has occurred to its supplier. It is not unreasonable that this type of situation should be covered. If a fire excuses performance, say, it doesn't really matter if the fire was at the provider's premises or one of its supplier's (as long as the fire at the supplier's premises does in fact have the knock-on effect on the service the customer is enjoying).

Secondly, when that supplier simply fails to perform (and not only for a force majeure reason). A provider would argue that their services are dependent on these third-party suppliers but that they are not able to control them and prevent failures. As such, they should be excused and not be held to have breached their contract with a customer (or held to have missed an SLA) if their supplier has let them down. A customer might well argue that it is open to the provider to include appropriate contractual provision in their contract with a supplier so that they have a remedy and can thereby pass the liability on. Whilst this is of course true, the provider would reply that its ability to recover from its supplier is likely to be limited given the inevitable existence of limitations and exceptions to liability.

To illustrate how this might occur in practice, let's take the example of a customer that acquires a SaaS service from a start-up provider that has built its offering on a PaaS solution. The PaaS provider may well be substantial and may offer service credits for availability issues to the start-up SaaS provider. However, if the SaaS provider is (in its contract with the customer) excused performance due to a failure of its suppliers, then even if the SaaS provider earns credits as a result of that failure it may well have no liability to its customer.[50] In this type of situation, availability of the service is very much in the hands of the subcontractor and if the SaaS provider is excused performance, there is little meaningful left in the provider's service level promise.

PRACTICAL TIP

A customer needs to pay particular attention to how the provider is excused performance due to a supplier (or subcontractor) default. This is especially so in contracts with start-up providers who have built their solutions on other cloud services.

At the very least, a customer will want to make sure that if its provider does recover compensation (whether in the form of service credits or otherwise) from a supplier, then it should have a right to have those (or an appropriate proportion of those) passed onto it.

---

[50] It should go without saying that this is all of course dependent on the precise contract language.

11.5.3 Customer

It is normal to excuse failures to meet service levels if the failure was caused by the customer itself.

11.6 Drafting issues around SLAs

Many cloud providers have developed a number of drafting techniques around service credits which if not designed to make it more difficult for a customer to claim certainly have that affect. We explore a few of these.

First, in any service contract some aspects can be relegated to a perhaps arbitrary status of 'operational detail', in relation to which a provider may reserve the right to change that detail. In cloud, this could be in relation to codes of conduct of use, support service details, or, to bring us back to the present context, service level details. Given the reliance a customer may have put on acquiring a service with, say, a particular level of availability, the concern is obvious: if the provider reserves the right to change that level, it may be changed to the customer's detriment going forward. A trap for the unwary is when the provider simply refers to the service level (or indeed any other 'operational detail') as being set out on a web page (or other non-signed document external to the actual contract) 'from time to time'. This latter expression means that the provider can change that detail.

> **PRACTICAL TIP**
>
> It is important that the customer is aware of whatever (if any) discretion the provider is reserving to amend the service levels during the term of the deal.

A service level needs to be monitored. Once a service level is monitored it needs to be reported on and the applicable credits then need to be applied. A cloud provider will of course inevitably monitor the performance of its own service and could if it wishes report on it to its customers and apply credits. This has a number of disadvantages for it. If the service is in fact down below the applicable level it may well be that a customer was not aware of it or at least not too concerned (the downtime could have been in a time that was not disruptive of the client's business). To report a problem to the customer will highlight service issues as well as damage revenue. As such, many cloud providers have adopted the practice of not reporting outages to its customers (but nonetheless making the information available through online means) and certainly not automatically applying service credits. Instead, a customer would need to request the application of a credit from the provider.

Whilst some cloud providers do offer the opportunity to check availability records of their particular 'instance' of the offering, others do not. Some providers require the customer itself to identify the lack of availability (through not being able to use the service) and to give documented evidence of it. Documented evidence required might consist of the customer's service logs. Even if the customer accepts that it has to monitor the availability and make its own claim for credits, the requirement for evidence needs to be carefully considered by the customer: will it always be able to provide evidence of a service failure?

Care is always needed in relation to the actual process required to trigger credits. Some providers, for example, require a customer, in order to obtain a credit, to report the start of the incident when the outage is ongoing and – according to this type of provision – the customer report defines the beginning of the outage period for the purpose of service credits. Accordingly, an incident that may in reality last a number of hours but is reported well into the incident will only have a correspondingly short 'official' outage period. Other cloud providers require a specific request to log or record the incident as an outage for service credit purposes. It is not, on the terms of these SLAs, sufficient simply to report the incident for the purpose of obtaining attention to the non-availability. These types of processes seem particularly unfair to the customer who in the midst of an outage is more likely to be concerned to get up and running again than to worry about financial compensation and the strict requirements set out in an SLA.

Providers will understandably want to set time limits within which a credit claim can be made. These are typically a number of days after the end of the relevant accounting period. The number of days can be relatively short (perhaps as little as 10 days). Whilst understandable from the provider's point of view, as it closes the incident, this is yet something else that a customer will need to have mechanisms in place to deal with.

From a customer perspective, what is best of course is the automatic reporting and application of service credits in accordance with the appropriate formula for calculation.

PRACTICAL TIP

A customer should consider requesting provisions in its contract requiring (i) the reporting on downtime and other service level issues; and (ii) the automatic application of credits to invoices.

11.7 Termination for failure to achieve service levels

A problem with a service credit regime as the sole remedy for service level failures is that it doesn't really offer the customer much if the provider is consistently obtaining a poor service, certainly, if the caps are low. It is entitled to some money back (but only by way of credit against invoices) or perhaps additional time for no charge. A cloud customer may find the service so bad that it wants to exit but finds that the SLA does not allow this; despite the poor quality the customer may be locked in for whatever period it signed up for as an initial term.

Contracts would normally have a general termination entitlement for a 'material' breach of contract. However, it is possible (depending on the precise wording) that this will not apply to service level issues if there is a provision which states that credits are the sole remedy.

PRACTICAL TIP

Customers should be aware that, if the service credit regime is expressed to be the sole remedy for service level failure, then the contract's general provision allowing for termination on certain types of breach may not apply.

Even if the general termination language did apply to a service failure issue, there could be an argument as to whether service level failure is the right type of breach. For these reasons, it would normally make sense for the customer to ensure there is an express termination right for service level failure. Thus, if the service failure is particular bad over a particular period, the customer can terminate. What is particularly bad for this purpose could be defined by a number of different criteria. The contract could provide that the client can terminate if the maximum service credits have been earned during any particular period. Alternatively, a right to terminate may arise where a maximum number of credits have been earned in a particular number of consecutive measurement periods or a particular number of measurement periods (not necessarily consecutive) over a year. Where there is more than one service level being measured, account needs to be taken of whether there should be a requirement that all metrics should have failed so as to reach the maximum credits for each of those metrics. As can be seen there are a number of possible permutations.

PRACTICAL TIP

A customer would consider including a termination entitlement at particularly bad service level failures. How bad will always be a matter for negotiation.

11.8 Key points

In this chapter we have explored service levels. Key points are as follows.

◆ Service level agreements are an important part of the overall contract and should always be carefully reviewed. They operate as an objective and measurable standard to which the service will be provided.

◆ There are usually consequences for the provider missing those standards, often the provision of credits against fees. These service credits are normally said to be the sole remedy a customer has (preventing an additional claim for damages) and may often be capped, however. The caps can sometimes be surprisingly low (as low as 10%). Once the cap is reached, there is often no further financial consequence for the provider in failing to provide the service to the appropriate level, although there will obviously be increasing loss of customer goodwill.

◆ In a typical cloud solution the 'availability' service level is the most important measure. Care is needed on how 'available' is defined when use by the customer might be over many different sites (and from perhaps many different provider 'instances' of the service). Another issue that needs care is the period of time over which service availability is measured.

◆ Target levels are aspirational; contractual levels have consequences.

◆ A customer should be wary of the provider seeking to reserve the right to amend the levels in the future.

◆ An attractive sounding level of availability needs to be considered in the context of the exceptions contained in the contract. Force majeure provisions can sometimes be very widely drawn. Another point for particular scrutiny is how the SLA deals with inabilities to provide services due to the fault of subcontractors. If the cloud provider is largely reliant on another provider (say, one of the major PaaS or IaaS providers) then there is probably little availability issue that is not the fault of one of those providers.

◆ Obligations to monitor and report need to be clearly allocated. Downtime of a service sometimes does not count as 'unavailability' for the purpose of credits until the customer has reported the fault. The processes around measurement and crediting are often complex. Generally, providers do not wish to make it easy for customers to earn credits.

◆ For repeated failures, or particularly serious isolated failures, to meet service levels a customer might consider seeking a right to terminate. As the service credit regime is often expressed to be the sole remedy for service level failure the contract's general provision allowing for termination on certain types of breach may well not apply. Tailored provisions should be negotiated.

12 Liability issues

12.1 Introduction

Cloud contracts, like any contract, can go wrong. There are many types of breaches that could occur in the cloud. There could be a lack of service availability. There could be problems with the functionality (bugs in the underlying software) so that wrong data is served up or calculations are incorrect. There may also be breaches of security so that the privacy of the customers' data is compromised or valuable trade secrets are lost. When any of these breaches occur, a customer can suffer losses and, subject to the terms of the contract, can seek to recover compensation for its losses from the provider. The calculation of the amount recoverable in court is based on the innocent party being entitled to be put in the same position it would have been in had the contract been properly performed. The loss that a user of a cloud service might suffer can easily become significant.

Given the multi-tenancy aspect of the typical cloud solution, if one customer suffers a breach of contract (such as a security breach) so too will many if not all of the other customers. As such, a breach of contract followed by many damages claim(s) could be fatal for the provider without the protection of wide-ranging exclusions and limitations, perhaps more so than in other outsourcing and managed services arrangements. Whilst a customer may well complain about needing to have the stick of large damages claims in order to incentivize the provider to perform diligently, a provider may remind the customer that there are other factors that operate as incentives, in particular the reputational damage to the provider if it is seen to breach the agreement or to not take its obligations seriously. Word will quickly spread if there are significant issues of contractual performance (especially given the possibility of multiple customers being affected) and this will be a big incentive to perform.

There are, broadly, two tools a provider will bring to bear to limit its exposure. First, it will make its obligations less than absolute by, for example, not guaranteeing all round availability, nor giving an absolute assurance that the software is bug free and/or will work, and so on. Timescales will seldom be absolute; the provider normally volunteering that it will 'use reasonable endeavours' to undertake particular tasks by a particular time. Security will be 'reasonable' or 'appropriate', and as such a breach of security will not necessarily be a breach of contract. In relation to availability, the provider will have set out its obligations in an SLA (see chapter 12). This type of language is designed to reduce the chances of the provider actually being in breach (even when from the viewpoint of the customer, the service is not fulfilling its needs).

Secondly, and normally in addition to the first tool, the provider will seek to include contractual language excluding certain legal rights that would normally arise for the benefit of the innocent party, that is, excluding certain losses or limiting liability for losses. A standard liability provision will include two parts: an absolute exclusion of certain types of losses (sometimes called indirect or consequential) and a cap on the liability of other (direct) losses which then remain recoverable up to that cap. Great care is always needed on the part of the customer as it is not uncommon for a provider to attempt to include within a list of losses, which have the appearance of 'indirect' losses, certain categories which might ordinarily under general legal principles be deemed 'direct'. It is not unknown for the 'cap' provision to have nothing really left to apply to as all conceivable losses have in fact already been excluded by what is called the 'consequential loss' provision.

PRACTICAL TIP

A customer should be aware that, whilst it may be considered standard and not (necessarily) unreasonable for certain types of losses such as 'indirect' losses to be excluded, the precise language may be widened to include within the exclusion losses which might on ordinary legal principles be considered direct (such as loss of data).[51]

Whatever the responsibility accepted by the provider, any contractual protection for the customer is only as good as the financial worth of the provider. If the provider is a start-up, has little by way of assets or substance, and subcontracts most of its offering, then that may not be the most suitable provider for a customer to use when outsourcing a critical part of its IT requirement.

12.2   Exclusions of liability

Certain types of losses are normally excluded in entirety in all contracts.

First, economic losses such as loss of profit or revenue, or loss of opportunity. This is intended amongst other things to prevent recovery of damages related to the inability of the cloud customer to carry on business if the service's failure (whether

---

[51]   See also the practical tip in Subclause 3.7.4.

unavailability or simply incorrect functioning) prevents it from doing so. If the cloud offering for example is related to providing the ability to trade, then trades that go wrong (profits that did not get made or losses that were not avoided) because the service failed would not be recoverable. Secondly, and more controversially, certainly in the cloud context, a provider may attempt in these clauses to exclude losses around data. Issues around liability for data are discussed in 3.7.4.

12.3   Limitations of liability

Any losses that are not excluded completely will inevitably be subject to contractual language under which the provider attempts to limit liability. There are many ways of structuring this but they all have one overriding objective – to put an absolute cap on the liability which the provider may have for breaching the contract. If the customer suffers losses above that cap, the customer can only recover the amount of the cap (to the extent it can prove under normal contract law principles the amount and the link between the loss and the breach). A rule of thumb has emerged that providers of IT services, hardware or software, will cap any liability that is accepted at the value of the contract. The rationale is that it should not accept any risk over the benefit to it of the particular contract (i.e. the value or price paid). What the 'value' is for this purpose can be drafted in a number of ways. The total liability over the life of the contract could be limited to the total amount paid over the full term. Alternatively, liability caps can operate on an annual basis so that in any year it can be limited to the amount paid in that year.

> **PRACTICAL TIP**
>
> Customers should always bear in mind that the figure set out in limitation of liability provisions is not an entitlement or an indication of the amount that will be obtained as a result of breach, only the maximum amount that could be claimed. A customer will still have to prove that there was a breach and that it caused the loss. It will also have to prove the amount of the loss that is suffered.
>
> Moreover, the service level agreement (SLA) will normally state in any case that liability for non-availability is only for the provider to pay the appropriate service credit (subject to all the exclusions in that SLA).

12.4   Chains of liability

A cloud provider that acquires components of its offering from another provider will not want to accept liability caused by that provider. For example, a SaaS provider, which has built its offering upon the platform or infrastructure of a large supplier such as Google or Amazon, will not want to accept liability for problems that are ultimately caused by its supplier. It is unlikely to have the same negotiating power with such giants as its customer may have with it. The provider therefore needs to strike a balance between the liability it can accept to customers for failure and the rights it has against its suppliers. This issue can be dealt with by the provider in a number of ways. First, the liability under the contract can be capped at a very low limit perhaps reflecting the value of the contract to it. If the provider can then negotiate a 'value' cap with its suppliers, there should be approximate correlation. Secondly, the issue might be dealt with by an express exclusion of liability stating that the supplier accepts no liability for losses caused by its suppliers. Such an approach could be wrapped up in a 'force majeure' clause (see also 11.5.1).

> **PRACTICAL TIP**
>
> A provider building its offering upon other cloud services will need to take a consistent approach in its contracts with customers. It needs to ensure that where appropriate it can pass liability onto its own suppliers.

12.5   Statutory and judicial control on liability exclusions

In the UK, contractual clauses that seek to exclude or restrict liability are subject to statutory control. There are two principal laws: the Unfair Contract Terms Act 1977 ('UCTA') [4], which applies to both business contracts and also consumer contracts, and the Unfair Terms in Consumer Contracts Regulations 1999 [30] (the 'Regulations'), which apply to consumer contracts only. A cloud provider preparing standard terms of business will need to be aware of these statutes and take them into account in its drafting.

12.5.1   *Unfair Contract Terms Act 1977*

In short, UCTA [4] restricts the ability of a party when contracting on its own standard terms or with consumers from excluding or limiting liability. In such situations, any attempt to exclude liability for breach of contract by the provider would be subject to a so-called 'reasonableness' test. The reasonableness test is whether the term is 'a fair and reasonable one ... having regard to the circumstances which were, or ought reasonably to have been, known to or in the contemplation of the parties when the contract was made'. The courts have applied a number of guidelines in judging what is reasonable including such considerations as to whether an inducement was offered to agree the limit, whether the parties had taken legal advice, the relative bargaining power of the parties and the availability of insurance.

PRACTICAL TIP

A cloud provider must be prepared to justify any limitation or exclusion of liability as 'reasonable'. Any complete exclusion of liability in relation to a cloud service that the customer pays for may well fall foul of this test, and a provider has to be prepared to accept some liability.

12.5.2 Unfair Terms in Consumer Contracts Regulations 1999

The Regulations complement UCTA [4]. They only apply to terms in contracts between a seller or supplier and a consumer (and not business-to-business contracts). A term is regarded as 'unfair' if it has not been individually negotiated and causes a significant imbalance in the positions of the parties to the detriment of the consumer in a way that is contrary to the requirements of good faith. The Regulations contain an 'indicative and non-exhaustive list' of terms regarded as unfair, a number of which may be particularly relevant to cloud providers. Any clause authorizing the supplier to terminate the contract at will where the same ability is not granted to the consumer and any clause allowing the supplier of services to increase the price without giving the consumer the corresponding right to cancel the contract will both be unfair.

Any clause which inappropriately excludes or limits the legal rights of the consumer in the event of inadequate performance by the supplier of any of the contractual obligations is unfair. Any attempt at excluding liability in entirety for lack of service availability will be within this prohibition. Of course, the key word is that the attempt at exclusion needs to be 'inappropriate' and it is not necessarily unfair to do so certainly when the service is made available to a consumer for free.

12.5.3 Attacks on supplier's standard terms

Given the prevalence of fairly aggressive limitation of liability provisions, often in small print in suppliers' terms, it is not surprising that these provisions feature in many reported court decisions relating to disputes following various IT supply agreements that have somehow gone wrong. The issue typically arises when a customer sues the provider for breach of contract (the system did not work) and the provider (as well as denying liability) then tries to rely on its contractual documentation to limit its exposure. The pendulum has swung back and forth over the last 15 years or so between judicial intervention, readily finding that supplier liability provisions were unreasonable in order to protect the 'small' customer, and a more permissive attitude recognizing that the parties themselves are the best placed people to decide what is reasonable or not. At present the pendulum is in favour of the supplier, perhaps permanently so.

We summarize some of the notable cases in the IT field. In the first few, clauses were repeatedly struck down. In *Salvage Association* v *CAP Financial Services*,[52] the contract was valued at £300,000 but contained a clause limiting CAP's liability to £25,000. The parties were of equal bargaining power and had taken legal advice. However, it was found that the clause was nonetheless unreasonable and therefore invalid. As a result, CAP's liability was unlimited. The court was swayed by a number of factors including that CAP had no evidence to justify the £25,000 limit in relation to the value of the contract or the financial risk taken by Salvage Association. CAP also had insurance which Salvage Association could not easily obtain. In *St Albans City and District Council* v *International Computers Limited*,[53] the contract contained a clause limiting ICL's liability to the lesser of the price or charge payable or £100,000. This clause was held to be unreasonable. Again, one of the factors taken into account importantly was that ICL could not justify the cap of £100,000 as well as the insurance position (a public sector body would find it hard to insure against commercial risks). In *Pegler Ltd* v *Wang (UK) Ltd*,[54] the court found it was unreasonable to rely on fairly standard exclusion of loss of profit liability when the supplier 'had so misrepresented what they were selling that breaches of contract were not unlikely'. In *Horace Holman Group* v *Sherwood International Group Ltd*,[55] a standard 'price paid' liability cap was struck down as being unreasonable.

All the cases just mentioned were very much in favour of the customer; clause after clause was struck down on the basis of an assessment by the courts that the terms were unreasonable. The tide turned in favour of the providers in 2001 with *Watford Electronics* v *Sanderson*.[56] The contract excluded liability for consequential loss and contained a 'price paid' limitation for other losses. The Court of Appeal upheld the clauses, stating that when parties of an equal bargaining power negotiate a contract so that the risk falls on one particular party, the courts should be 'cautious' about saying that a term is not reasonable. This was such an important turning point in the application of UCTA [4] to business cases and a marked departure from the earlier judicial interventionism that it is worth quoting one of the more important passages in the judgement:

> Where experienced businessmen representing substantial companies of equal bargaining power negotiate an agreement, they may be taken to have had regard to the matters known to them. They should, in my view be taken to be the best judge of the commercial fairness of the agreement which they

52 1995 FSR 654. Salvage Association v. CAP Financial Services Ltd [1995] FSR 654
53 1996 4 All ER 481. See: http://www.bailii.org/ew/cases/EWCA/Civ/1996/1296.html
54 2000 Build L R 248. See: http://www.bailii.org/ew/cases/EWHC/TCC/2000/137.html
55 2002 EWCA Civ 170. See: http://www.bailii.org/ew/cases/EWCA/Civ/2002/170.html
56 2001 All ER 290. See: http://www.bailii.org/ew/cases/EWCA/Civ/2001/317.html

have made; including the fairness of each of the terms in that agreement. They should be taken to be the best judge on the question whether the terms of the agreement are reasonable. The court should not assume that either is likely to commit his company to an agreement which he thinks is unfair, or which he thinks includes unreasonable terms. Unless satisfied that one party has, in effect, taken unfair advantage of the other – or that a term is so unreasonable that it cannot properly have been understood or considered – the court should not interfere.

As a result of this decision, cloud providers should be more confident that their clauses should survive scrutiny.[57]

PRACTICAL TIP

A cloud provider must be prepared to justify any limitation or exclusion of liability as 'reasonable'; and pegging the cap on liability for direct losses to the value of the contract is one approach which should work.

12.5.4 The danger of overselling

A very recent case, *BSkyB Ltd* v *HP Enterprise Services UK Ltd* (formerly Electronic Data Systems Ltd),[58] has introduced another possible element of attack. If a supplier deliberately oversells its product when it knows it will not do what the customer wants, it will be hard for it to rely on protective contractual language. BSkyB engaged Electronic Data Systems Ltd (EDS) to build a customer relationship management system. The contract had a value of £47.6 million and contained a limitation of liability clause which capped EDS' liability at £30 million. EDS never delivered and BSkyB ended up building the system itself and sued EDS for £706 million of losses. The customer (BSkyB), who suffered substantial losses, could not attack the limitation language on the basis of UCTA [4] as the contract was not on the standard terms of the supplier. It successfully brought a claim for 'fraudulent misrepresentation' as one of its managing directors had made statements to BSkyB which he knew were false or at the very least was reckless as to whether they were true or not. These statements included confirming that EDS had fully scoped the work and that the timescales were realistic even though it had not carried out any supporting analysis. The £30 million cap on liability was of no assistance to EDS as it expressly did not apply in the event of fraud. Once liability was determined, the parties agreed a figure for damages of £318 million in June 2010.

---

[57] Clauses can still fail, however. In *Kingsway Hall Hotel Ltd* v *Red Sky IT (Hounslow) Ltd* [2010] EWHC 965, the High Court struck down a fairly typical exclusion clause. See: http://www.bailii.org/ew/cases/EWHC/TCC/2010/965.html

[58] 2010 EWHC 86 (TCC). See: http://www.bailii.org/ew/cases/EWHC/TCC/2010/86.html

It is a salutary reminder to suppliers not to over-promise in the tender process as such promises can lead to liability even if they are not then confirmed in a written contract.

12.6   Key points

In this chapter we explored the issue of provider liability and contractual exclusions. Key points are as follows.

◆ Any service contract produced as a standard form by a provider (cloud or otherwise) will contain exclusions and limitations on liability. The nature of a cloud service is that if there is a failure of the service many customers are likely to be affected. Losses that are suffered by users could (if they were passed on to providers) be concentrated to levels jeopardizing the existence of the provider.

◆ Liability is limited in a number of ways. First, service credits are sometimes said to be the sole remedy for failure. Secondly, obligations are often not absolute but qualified by a requirement to use 'reasonable' efforts so that there is only liability if that standard is not met. Thirdly, the type of loss which can be recovered if there is liability under these types of reduced standards is then limited to certain types of losses (other losses, such as 'indirect' losses or perhaps 'loss of data' being excluded). Lastly, the damages that are not so excluded are then capped at a particular financial level.

◆ Any contractual protection for the customer is only as good as the financial worth of the provider. A customer outsourcing the custody of valuable data needs always to be aware of the financial and organization substance of its chosen cloud provider.

◆ When much of the offering is subcontracted by the provider, it needs to strike a balance between the liability it can accept to customers for failure and the rights it has against its suppliers.

◆ A cloud provider preparing standard terms of business will need to be aware of statutory control on exclusion clauses. In the UK, UCTA [4] requires terms to be reasonable and the Unfair Terms in Consumer Contract Regulations [30] requires (when dealing with consumers) terms to be fair.

◆ The latest court decisions indicate that (certainly in business to business contracts) there will be little scope for attacking terms on these grounds unless they are particularly unreasonable. Nonetheless, it is likely that some liability should be accepted when the service is not a free one; and a rule of thumb pegging the level to the value of the contract should work.

13 Specific sectors

13.1 Introduction

Up to this point we have considered cloud services in a general sense; customers acquiring them could be in any sector. Many customers of course operate in sectors where there exist specific regulatory frameworks in relation to their activities, and these frameworks may contain legal requirements relevant to a specific cloud deployment.

In this chapter we consider the legal consequences that arise from certain specific sectors: financial services, cloud services provided to consumers and cloud in the public sector.

13.2 Financial services

13.2.1 Introduction to the regulatory regime

The financial sector of course is heavily regulated and there are a number of international requirements that are required to be fulfilled by those operating in that sector, both substantive legal requirements and requirements imposed by regulators such as the Financial Services Authority (FSA).[59] The legal framework in the UK is primarily under the Financial Services & Markets Act 2000 (FSMA) [31]. Under section 19 of FSMA, any person who carries on a regulated activity in the UK must be authorized by the FSA (unless they are exempt). It is a criminal offence not to be.

Firms that are authorized by the FSA are required to comply with rules set out by the FSA, which were extensively revised in respect of outsourcing to bring the UK into line with its international obligations arising out of the European Union's MiFID Directive [32]. There are no specific requirements on the topic of cloud services, but those guidelines which apply to outsourcing generally are certainly wide enough to cover cloud services.

---

[59] The new coalition government has announced that the FSA will be disbanded in 2012, with its powers and responsibilities then vested in other regulators, including the Bank of England.

The FSA regime makes distinctions between rules which apply to banks, building societies and investment companies and then rules which apply to insurers. There are also rules which apply generally to all entities (in financial services terminology, 'firms'), all of which we explore in this section.

13.2.2   Generally applicable rules – FSA Principles of Business

The rules are set out in the FSA Handbook [28] which contains both general 'Principles of Business' and also specific rules which may have application to the cloud. All regulated firms have an obligation to manage their affairs in accordance with Principle 3 (Management and Control). This requires the firm to take reasonable care to organize and control its affairs responsibly and effectively, with adequate risk management systems.

There is also an extremely general and all pervasive principle on the relationship with regulators (Principle 11) which requires the regulated firm to deal with its regulators in an open and cooperative way. A firm must disclose to the FSA anything relating to the firm of which the FSA would reasonably expect notice. Guidance from the FSA requires the firm to take reasonable steps to ensure that a similar obligation on cooperation is imposed upon any service provider to which a material aspect of the firm's function has been outsourced. This will include the provision of data and information.

Moreover, guidance to Principle 11[60] states that if an outsourcing is material (defined to be of such importance that weakness, or failure, of the services would cast serious doubt upon the firm's continuing compliance with the rules), the FSA should be informed of the outsourcing.

There are other more specific rules that impact upon a firm's ability to outsource any aspect of its function. None focus on cloud services, but there are requirements focused on outsourcing generally, mostly set out in different parts of 'the Senior Management Arrangements, Systems and Controls sourcebook (SYSC)'. One important rule in this sourcebook, applicable to all firms, is SYSC 3.1.1: 'A firm must take reasonable care to establish and maintain such systems and controls as are appropriate to its business'.

13.2.3   Banks, building societies and investment firms

Certain regulated financial institutions (called in the rules 'common platform firms',[61] but including banks, building societies and other investment firms) are obliged to comply with the rules set out in the outsourcing provision of the SYSC

---

[60]   FSA Handbook [28], SUP 15.3.8.
[61]   A firm subject to the Capital Requirements Directive (CRD) [33] or MiFID [32] or both.

rule 8. Other regulated firms (not 'common platform firms') should have regard to these provisions as if they were a guidance not a requirement.

SYSC 8 focuses on the outsourcing of operational functions that are 'critical' or 'important' (these terms are probably alternatives; although both are used, there is not thought to be any difference in their meaning).[62] These are functions where a defect or failure in performance would materially impair the continuing compliance with the conditions and obligations of the firm's FSA authorization or its other obligations under the regulatory system, or its financial performance, or the soundness or the continuity of its relevant services and activities. Where a function that is to be outsourced to a cloud provider is critical or important, it should be noted that there is no prohibition on engaging that cloud provider, only a requirement to take additional care. SYSC 8.1.1 stipulates that the firm, when engaging a provider (cloud or otherwise) to provide a service that is critical or important, should take reasonable steps to avoid undue additional operational risk. It should also not engage that provider in such a way as to impair materially the quality of the firm's internal controls and the ability of the FSA to monitor the firm's compliance with all obligations under the regulatory system.

Some typical cloud services may well be automatically deemed not to be critical or important as a result of SYSC 8.1.5, paragraph (2), which reads 'the purchase of standardised services, including market information services and the provision of price feeds'. The full width of the term 'standardized' may lead to surprising consequences. Most cloud services are indeed standardized (in that they are not tailored for a particular customer) and that is true for both SaaS and IaaS solutions. We come back to this in 13.2.4.

If the cloud provision is a critical or important function then other parts of SYSC 8 need to be considered. SYSC 8.1.7 requires a common platform firm to exercise due skill and care and diligence when entering into, managing or terminating any arrangement for the outsourcing to a service provider of such a function. SYSC 8.1.8 elaborates and sets out a number of more specific tasks, some of which in reality are no more than sensible commercial provisions that any customer would want to put in place. The firm must ensure that the service provider has the ability and capacity to perform the services reliably and professionally. It must put in place methods for assessing the standard of performance of the service provider and properly supervise the performance. It is required to take appropriate action if it appears that the service provider may not be performing. It should contain in the contract an obligation to ensure that the service provider discloses to the firm any development that may have a material impact on its ability to carry out the services properly. The firm should have regard to exit arrangements (to ensure that the provision can be terminated

---

[62] Indeed, there is probably no difference between these terms and the term 'material outsourcing' used elsewhere in the rules.

without detriment to the continuity and quality of its servicing of its own clients). The service provider should be obliged to protect confidential data. The firm (with the service provider) needs to maintain disaster recovery plans and back-up facilities.

Lastly, two other relevant provisions: rule SYSC 8.1.9 requires a written contract to be entered into, whilst SYSC 8.1.12 requires the firm to notify the FSA when critical or important functions are being outsourced.

13.2.4 Investment firms using cloud services

Much of the SYSC 8 requirements which have just been summarized are what a well advised and prudent cloud customer would be doing in any case: undertaking diligence in relation to the provider's ability, monitoring and reporting, exit planning, and so on. This should be done by any (even non-regulated) customer.

Some provisions might present more difficulty. In particular, the firm is required to ensure that the service provider cooperates with the FSA and it is hard to see how the average cloud provider (certainly a non-UK provider) would agree to cooperate with the FSA. Likewise, the firm should ensure that it, its auditors and the FSA have effective access to data and audit rights. As such, it is difficult to see any regulated firm outsourcing 'critical or important' functions to the cloud except where the cloud provider is specializing in providing services to UK financial services clients and is giving an assurance that the data will remain in the UK so that the premises and data can be accessed by the FSA.

It is therefore important (if the data will not remain in the UK) for a customer to get comfortable that a cloud service is not 'critical or important'. This topic is addressed in industry guidelines from 2007. MiFID Connect is a grouping of UK trade associations set up to advise its members on compliance with MiFID [32] generally. In 2007, they produced guidelines on outsourcing[63] which have been sanctioned by the FSA (the FSA has said that it will take these guidelines into account when exercising its regulatory functions). This document states that the following are likely to constitute outsourcing within the rules and *potentially* (although not definitely) outsourcings of critical or important functions:

a) provision of data storage (physical and electronic);

b) provision of ongoing, day-to-day systems maintenance/support; and

c) provision of ongoing, day-to-day software/systems management, e.g. where a third party carries out day-to-day functionality and/or runs software or processes on its own systems.

---

[63] Guideline on the Application of the Outsourcing Requirements under the FSA Rules Implementing MiFID [32] and the CRD [33] in the UK.

All of these functions could be acquired through the cloud. Whilst they are potentially critical or important, the same guidelines also state that where the outsourced function is only one of many manners in which the service can be provided, it would not be considered critical where a failure in relation to one manner would not affect the firm's ability to operate. Thus if data storage is acquired as a cloud service, it would be critical or important if the firm were using that service provider only, but not (or at least not necessarily so) when it is merely one of a number of storage solutions (say for back-up).

PRACTICAL TIP

Financial services firms need to consider whether a particular cloud service is or may be critical or important. If so, or if there is doubt as to whether it might be, the additional controls set out in SYSC 8 should be applied, including by means of appropriate contractual language.

In particular, they will need to ensure that they obtain assurances from the cloud provider to cooperate with the FSA and to keep data in the UK.

Lastly, any acquisition of a cloud service (of a critical or important type) leads to an obligation to inform the FSA.

13.2.5 Insurance companies

As mentioned above, companies in the insurance sector are subject to a different set of FSA rules. The main rules in this sector are set out in SYSC 13, and in particular SYSC 13.9 on outsourcing. SYSC 14 (Prudential risk management and associated systems and controls for insurers) is also relevant.

SYSC 13 provides guidance to insurers in relation to their systems and controls for managing risks concerning any of their operations, including their IT systems. Whilst much of the guidance is relevant to outsourcing, there is specific guidance on outsourcing in SYSC 13.9. The guidance re-emphasizes that an insurer should take reasonable care to supervise the discharge of outsourced functions. It also restates the guidance mentioned above that a firm should notify the FSA when it intends to enter into a material outsourcing arrangement.

There are recommendations targeted at the pre-contract stage. The insurer should undertake due diligence in relation to the service provider and should consider how the arrangement will fit into its risk profile and business strategy, paying particular attention to what will happen on the termination of the contract.

As with investment firms outsourcing critical functions, the FSA requires the insurer to put written contracts in place. Regard should be had to appropriate monitoring and appropriate contractual protection. Again, there should be sufficient access available to the insurer's auditors and to the FSA. A service level agreement is advised, and that should contain appropriate performance targets to assess the adequacy of service provisions. Service delivery should be evaluated through service delivery reports and periodic self-certification or independent review by auditors. An insurer should ensure that it has appropriate business continuity arrangements for the possibility of a loss of services.

The rules expressly recognize that an insurer may find it beneficial to use externally validated reports commissioned by the service provider, to seek comfort as to the adequacy and effectiveness of its systems and controls.[64] Nonetheless, the use of such reports will not absolve the insurer of responsibility nor remove the need to have its own right to access premises.

SYSC 14 requires an insurer to take reasonable steps to have an adequate risk management system, to document its policy for operational risk and how it monitors and controls that risk, and to have in place adequate internal controls.

13.2.6 *Insurers using cloud services*

Insurers have greater leeway to enter into a cloud service than banks, building societies and investment firms. Whilst the latter have to comply with mandatory rules in relation to critical or important functions, insurers when outsourcing are required only to have regard to the relevant guidance – it is less prescriptive. Nonetheless, the same difficulties that were mentioned for investment firms, in relation to preserving access rights for both the customer and the regulator, would exist here.

13.3 Cloud in the public sector

Even before the change of government in May 2010 and issues of cutting budget deficit, the UK government had been considering the benefits of cloud computing. The Digital Britain report of 2009 contained a call that 'all those Government bodies likely to procure ICT services should look to do so on a scalable, cloud basis ...', giving the cloud momentum additional credibility. Government should share in the well-known benefits of cloud: adopting cloud computing, the report said, 'substantially cuts hardware and application costs and allows much more rapid product and service innovation'. Indeed, given the size of the public sector IT spend, a major adoption of cloud technologies (perhaps more of the 'private cloud' type) can be expected in the near future.

The UK is not alone here. At the time of writing the most prominent incidence of a public cloud was the signing of a contract in December 2009 by the City of Los

---

[64] See 3.5 and 3.6.

Angeles with Google, under which LA acquired cloud email services. The contract was made public as a result of rules on public freedom of information.

Most legal issues around cloud adoption apply equally in the public sector as they do in the private sector. Public entities need to worry about service levels, service descriptions/changes, information security and so on just as much as entities in the private sector. One legal issue that does not arise in the private sector is that of public procurement rules.

A full discussion of the public procurement rules is outside the scope of this book (and reference could be made to the standard texts). Suffice to say that when a public authority acquires any goods, works or services above a certain threshold an open (and published) process needs to be followed. The intention of the rules is to open up the market to competition throughout Europe. There are separate rules and thresholds depending on whether the contract is for goods, works or services. Whilst the acquisition of hardware would be within the 'goods' rules, cloud services (including the acquisition of server capacity as an IaaS) would, if caught at all, be within the 'services' rules, in England and Wales, in the Public Contracts Regulations 2006 [34] (which implement a directive from 2004).

The public sector for this purpose includes central government departments, local government, NHS trusts, police and fire authorities, national museums, various quangos and so on. The threshold for services depends on the type of services, but cloud services are likely to be 'Part A' services (certain services which have an international appeal)[65] for which the current threshold is €125,000 (for central government) and €193,000 (for other public sector bodies). IT services (and so cloud services) are Part A services.

If a public authority is acquiring IT services with a value above these thresholds, the process set out in the Regulations needs to be followed. This process includes an obligation to advertise the contract, prescribed rules on the minimum number of tenderers being invited fully into one of the three alternative processes, and a requirement for the decision-making process to be transparent. The public body must award the contract to the tender that has the lower price or, alternatively, that is the 'most economically advantageous tender (MEAT)' (which can take into account other factors such as quality and technical aspects). The relative weighting of the MEAT factors needs to be part of the tender documentation.

One final legal aspect which cloud providers should be aware of: contracts entered into with public authorities may be subject to Freedom of Information Act 2000 (FOIA) [35] and so come into the public domain. Any person, such as the media or competitors, can submit a request under the FOIA to a public sector body to disclose

---

[65] Part B services are those that are likely to be of interest only to suppliers in the same country as the public authority.

the widest class of information (including contracts that have been awarded and service reports provided and so on). There are exemptions where the information is a trade secret or held in confidence, but these are high thresholds. There are some practical steps that a cloud provider can take to maximize the chance that one of these exemptions will apply (for example, to include pricing or proprietary information which is a trade secret in a separate schedule clearly labelled as such and to contractually require the public authority to consult with the provider). Reference should be made to the standard texts on the topic. (The Google/Los Angeles contract referred to previously has been made public with full commercial terms under the US equivalent of the UK's FOIA.)

13.4 Consumer cloud

13.4.1 Introduction

Many consumer applications on the internet are cloud services (at least, if you take the widest meaning of that term). Consumers using such services as email (e.g. Gmail and Hotmail), social networking sites (e.g. Facebook) and media sharing sites (e.g. YouTube and Flickr) are all entrusting their data to software applications acquired remotely and in a scalable fashion, and the consumer has no idea at all where the data is. These are all examples of software as a service. There are also more 'infrastructure'-like services available for consumers such as data back-up and storage sites (e.g. Dropbox), but to the extent it makes any difference these too are really best characterized as SaaS since the consumer is not 'building' anything onto the infrastructure.

The consumer of course makes a decision about using a cloud service in a somewhat different way to an enterprise. Concerns such as security standards, due diligence, service level commitments, the terms of the contract (which are never negotiable) are not normally in the forefront of a consumer's mind. And this is so even when services are paid for. A consumer is unlikely to compare, for example, different providers' stances on liability issues. A decision will be made on the basis of functionality, usability of the service and to a certain extent fashion and peer pressure.

In this section we examine a few other legal issues that arise in the consumer cloud environment. Many of the consumer cloud services allow a consumer to upload content (perhaps for wider dissemination) and so one legal issue that arises is whether and to what extent a provider might be held liable for that type of hosting. Next we look at liability. In chapter 12 we looked at liability issues generally (which arise with a different flavour here) including statutory control over the extent to which a provider can exclude liability for its own breach. Lastly, we look at how the data protection rules (covered extensively in chapter 4) apply when the provider is selling to consumers.

13.4.2   Liability of a cloud provider for hosting user content

Introduction

Many cloud services (especially those – but not exclusively – targeted to consumers) involve the provider hosting on the internet content created or uploaded by the user. In doing so, a cloud provider risks liability for the actions of its users. In an attempt to shield themselves from liability, cloud providers will generally have terms (sometimes in a separate document called an Acceptable Use Policy or 'AUP') which sets out what customers can do with the service. Nevertheless, such providers remain a more attractive target for a potential claimant than the user who may not have the same level of financial resources and may be more difficult to trace. This section examines the extent of this potential liability and how it can in practice be avoided.

There are a number of potential liability risks that a cloud provider leaves itself open to as a result of content put up by its users. In many cases, European cloud providers will have a general defence under the Ecommerce Directive [5], which is where we begin.

Defence under the Ecommerce Directive

Electronic Commerce (EC Directive) Regulations 2002 [36] (the 'Ecommerce Regulations') implement the Ecommerce Directive (2000/31/EC) [5] in the UK. Regulation 19 of the Ecommerce Regulations provides a 'hosting' defence available to providers of 'information society services', which will include the type of cloud service being considered here. This provision states that where a service consists of the storage of information provided by a user (that is, uploaded content), the provider will not be liable where the service provider does not have actual knowledge of unlawful activity or information and is not aware of facts or circumstances from which it would have been apparent to the service provider that the activity or information was unlawful. Where the provider discovers the unlawful activity or information (perhaps as a result of a rights holder informing it), the provider avoids liability if it acts expeditiously to remove or disable access to the information (a so-called, 'notice and takedown' process).

PRACTICAL TIP

A cloud provider allowing users to upload content should reserve the right under its contract to remove that content in certain circumstances (such as when a complaint arrives).

It should also ensure that in the contract, the user indemnifies the provider in relation to any liability.

As mentioned, this process is a general provision applicable to many different types of potentially unlawful activity. We now consider some specific types of potential liability for consumer content.

Copyright infringement

If content is uploaded into a cloud service, the copyright of which is not owned by the user, the provider will also potentially be infringing copyright.[66]

To date, the most well-known examples of this type of liability have arisen in the US. Viacom unsuccessfully sued YouTube and its owner Google in the US courts[67]. In March 2007 it claimed compensation of US$1 billion for infringement of copyright in videos posted on the YouTube site. Viacom had argued that Google did not qualify for immunity under the Digital Millennium Copyright Act 1998 [37], which provides a hosting defence similar in intention to that in the Ecommerce Directive, because internal records showed that Google was well aware that its video-hosting site was riddled with infringing material posted by its users. In essence, Viacom argued that general awareness of infringing acts were enough. Google contended that it needed *specific* notice of each infringement and that it had indeed complied with thousands of takedown notices from Viacom. Google prevailed in a judgement given in June 2010. At the time of writing it was reported that an appeal would be made.

In the UK, likewise, a service provider may well be able to rely on the hosting defence of the Ecommerce Regulations.

Trademark infringement

There are two main ways in which online service providers can be liable for trade mark infringement: when a user puts a third party trade mark into the service as an advertising 'key word' and when a user attempts to sell infringing goods. Two recent cases (albeit not involving services that can properly be called cloud) show that it will be hard for the service provider to be held liable.

---

[66] This would be as a result of either 'reproducing' the work (whether or not it is further disseminated or made available) when it is stored on servers and so on or by communicating the work to the public when other users can access it, both of which are 'restricted acts' under the Copyright, Designs and Patents Act 1988.

[67] *Viacom International Inc and others. v. YouTube Inc and others*, 07 Civ. 2103 (LLS) US District Court for the Southern District of New York, 23 June 2010. See: http://www.eff.org/files/filenode/viacom_v_youtube/06-23-10_Summary_Judgment.pdf

In the recent *Google France* v *Louis Vuitton*,[68] a number of trade mark owners, including Louis Vuitton, sued Google France for trade mark infringement on the basis of the use of their trade marks as sponsored key words. The European Court of Justice (ECJ) held that Google could not be liable for trade mark infringement because the provision of its AdWords tool did not amount to use of a third-party mark in the course of trade for various technical reasons which are outside the scope of this book. However, it also found that the hosting defence of the Ecommerce Directive only applies where the service provider's role was 'neutral, in the sense that its conduct is merely technical, automatic and passive, pointing to a lack of knowledge or control' of the key word data that it stored from the advertiser. Once the provider becomes aware of the infringing nature of the stored data or the advertiser's activities it must act expeditiously to remove or disable access to the data in order to avoid liability.

In *L'Oreal SA* v *eBay*,[69] the English High Court held that eBay was not jointly liable with individual sellers for the sale of infringing or counterfeit products on its auction site. It held that eBay was under no legal duty or obligation to prevent infringement of third parties' registered trade marks. It stated that eBay did facilitate the infringement of third-party trade marks by its sellers; it knew that such infringements had occurred and were likely to continue to occur; and it profited from such infringements. However, these factors were not enough to make eBay jointly liable.

Defamation

Anyone who participates in the publication of defamatory material is treated as having caused its publication. A cloud provider hosting user content is potentially liable for anything defamatory that the user posts. The main defence available to service providers is that of innocent dissemination under the Defamation Act 1996 [38]. To rely on this the service provider must show that (i) it is not the author, editor or publisher of the relevant statement, (ii) it took reasonable care in relation to its publication, and (iii) it did not know, and had no reason to believe, that what it did caused or contributed to the publication of a defamatory statement.

A cloud provider will not be considered to be an author, editor or publisher if it is only involved as a provider of services without exerting any editorial control. However, if the provider exerts that control, it may lose the benefit of the defence. Also, if it decides neither to monitor content on its site nor to respond to complaints,

---

[68] *Google France SARL and Google Inc.* v *Louis Vuitton Malletier SA, Google France and Google Inc.* v *Viaticum SA,* and *Google France and Google Inc.* v *CNRRH,* Joined Cases C-236/08, C-237/08 and C-238/08, 23 March 2010. See: http://eur-lex.europa.eu/LexUriServ/LexUriServ.do?uri= OJ:C:2010:134:0002:0003:EN:PDF

[69] *L'Oreal SA* v *eBay International AG* 2009 EWHC 1094 (Ch). See: http://www.bailii.org/ew/cases/EWHC/Ch/2009/1094.html

it may breach the requirement to take reasonable care in relation to its publication of the offending statement. Thus, as with the Ecommerce Regulations (which would also in any case apply), if material is taken down, the provider should avoid liability.

Other illegal content

There are a whole range of other unlawful acts which a cloud provider might unwittingly be implicated in as a result of content posted by a user. For example, it is a criminal offence to publish, disseminate or display written material where it is intended or likely to stir up racial or religious hatred. A provider can avoid conviction if (as would be likely when it is merely hosting) it can show that it was not aware of the content of the material and did not suspect, and had no reason to suspect, that it was unlawful. Providers can also rely on the 'mere hosting' defence under the Ecommerce Regulations to avoid liability.

Providers also face a risk that users will upload inappropriate or illegal content that includes obscene or classified content and child pornography. Such content is governed by a number of key criminal law statutes (for example, the Obscene Publications Act 1959 [39], the Protection of Children Act 1978 [40] and the Criminal Justice Act 1988 [41]). Content may also be inappropriate for minors. The use of age verification software to separate adult content from other content could reduce the risk that material is considered obscene, as the target audience is restricted. Primary defences of innocent publication are available in some circumstances. However, where these might not be available, providers may, again, be able to rely on the 'mere hosting' defence.

Some statutes have special provisions dealing with internet activities (and defences). Regulation 7 of the Electronic Commerce Directive (Terrorism Act 2006) Regulations 2007 [42], for example, mirrors the 'mere hosting' defence' of the Ecommerce Regulations. It provides a defence for service providers to certain terrorism offences in respect of a service that consists of the storage of information provided by a user if (broadly) the provider did not know when the information was provided that it was terrorism-related, or upon obtaining actual knowledge that it was, the service provider expeditiously removed the information or disabled access to it.

Conclusion on user content hosting

Any cloud provider hosting user content will always run the risk of unwittingly committing some unlawful act as a result of the user's actions. Clearly, AUPs, warranties and indemnities can – in theory – provide protection to a provider. However, in practice such protection is often worthless. It will not normally be possible to identify the real person behind the user account (certainly for free services where credit card details are not obtained), and in any case private individuals will often not be worth pursuing through courts.

13.4.3   Liability under contracts with consumers

Any contractual limitation or exclusion of liability can only be relied on if it can be successfully assessed against the 'reasonableness' test of the Unfair Contract Terms Act 1977 [4] and the 'fairness' test under the Unfair Terms in Consumer Contracts Regulations [30] 1999 (see chapter 12). The fact that a service may be free of charge will assist in ensuring that any such assessment is in the provider's favour, but it will not be determinative. Indeed, an exclusion of all liability for failure to provide services may well survive scrutiny when the service is free.

Liability for data in consumer contracts is a little bit more complex. A distinction needs to be made between liability for breach of security of data (that is, when the data gets into the wrong hands) and liability for loss of data (that is, when data is simply deleted). In the respect of the former, a provider is unlikely to be able to hide behind exclusions in relation to questions of data breach as there are statutory obligations under the Data Protection Act [16] which cannot be overridden by contractual language. However, that is not the case in relation to loss of data and an attempt to exclude liability for failing to keep the data (certainly in a free service) may well be reasonable and fair. Consumers will therefore need to ensure that they have an alternative repository of any valuable data they have stored in a cloud service.

In short, liability for availability can probably be avoided, as can liability for loss of data, with carefully drafted contractual terms. However, a provider will always be potentially liable for breach of security as a result of data protection law.

13.4.4   Data protection with consumers

Any business (cloud or not) dealing with consumers will have complex data protection issues to deal with. The business will have to comply with the data protection principles and other rules summarized in chapter 4. A SaaS provider targeting consumers has to take appropriate security steps, it has to use data only for purposes for which it was collected, it has to (unless exempt) register with the ICO, and so on.

However, some of issues that arise because the business is operating in the consumer cloud can in fact be simpler to deal with than in the business cloud. We discussed in chapter 4 such issues as: which of the cloud customer or the cloud provider is the 'data controller', with the associated data protection responsibilities; how the customer can lawfully transfer data to a non-EU cloud provider; and how the customer can, in compliance with their data protection obligations, ensure that proper security is in place. These issues do not really arise, or at least not in the same way, in a consumer cloud situation; the provider is clearly a data controller. If the provider is 'established' within the UK,[70] it has to comply with the Data Protection Act.

If a UK-based SaaS provider uses in turn an IaaS or PaaS service provider, who might be located outside the UK, it is no different from any enterprise putting its customers' data into the cloud; all the issues summarized in chapters 5 and 6 apply equally here. It makes no difference that the data is 'consumer data' collected as part of a cloud service; the cloud provider is also in turn a cloud customer.

Lastly, it is true that regulators have taken a particular interest in relation to some of the issues that arise for the provider when selling services to consumers. There is an opinion from the Article 29 Working Party, for example, on data protection in the social networking arena [43]. In the first half of 2010, moreover, the privacy practices of Facebook and Google were under particular scrutiny, including in relation to the default 'privacy settings' they have on their sites.

PRACTICAL TIP

Cloud service providers handling consumer personal data have a particular need to be careful in complying with data protection rules.

13.5 Key points

In this chapter we have explored issues that arise in specific sectors (financial services, the public sector and consumers). Key points are as follows.

- Entities in the financial services sector are subject to regulation that might impact upon their freedom to use cloud services. The FSA is entitled to be informed of any material outsourcings that regulated entities undertake.

- The FSA sets out requirements that apply when 'common platform firms' (which include banks, building societies and other investment firms) outsource

---

[70] See 4.5.2.

'critical' or 'important' functions. Some of the functions which might be outsourced to the cloud (such as data storage) could fall into this category, in which case the FSA requirements must be adhered to. However, many of these rules are what any prudent cloud customer would be doing in any case.

◆ Some of the requirements will be difficult to comply with except (perhaps) where the cloud provider is specializing in providing services to UK financial services clients. The firm is required (for 'critical' or 'important' functions) to ensure that the cloud service provider cooperates with the FSA and that the FSA has effective access to data and audit rights.

◆ Insurance companies are not 'common platform firms' and have greater leeway to enter into a cloud service. There are no mandatory rules even in relation to critical or important functions, only guidance. Nonetheless, they face the same difficulties in relation to preserving access rights for both the customer and the regulator.

◆ Legal issues around cloud adoption in the public sector are largely the same as in the private sector. One novel issue is that of public procurement rules which public authorities will always need to adhere to when the value of a cloud contract is over a particular value.

◆ Many consumer applications on the internet are examples of SaaS. Consumer services that allow a consumer to upload content give rise to the potential possibility of a provider being held liable for anything unlawful in that content. Many of the wrongs for which a provider might inadvertently be liable are subject to a defence under the Ecommerce Directive [5] if a 'notice and takedown' process is applied.

◆ Contracts with consumers should always reserve the right for the provider to remove/take down content. Indemnities are standard but when there is a difficulty even in identifying the real person behind the account let alone be certain as to whether that person has substance to put behind an indemnity, their usefulness is doubtful.

◆ Contracts with consumers should also contain protection in relation to claims a consumer might bring against the cloud provider. Any limitation language needs to be 'reasonable' and also 'fair' to be enforceable under UK law. Breach of data protection rules cannot be excluded.

◆ Cloud service providers handling consumer personal data (in particular social networking sites) are being carefully scrutinized by regulators in Europe and so have a particular need to be careful in complying with data protection rules.

14 The future of cloud law

14.1 Introduction

As will have been seen throughout this book, the predominant feature of the legal landscape in the cloud is the application of familiar legal principles to an unfamiliar terrain. Cloud as a model has evolved out of earlier structures for the sale of computing functionality and infrastructure, and the legal principles that sufficed for those earlier structures are being made to apply to the new models. There is as yet no such independent body of 'cloud law'.

We conclude this book by briefly speculating on how that landscape may change in the medium to long term, as well as dealing with a number of initiatives that seek to make it easier for customers to contract for the cloud.

14.2 Open cloud

As noted elsewhere in this book,[71] one of the critical issues with contracting for the cloud is the ability of the customer to retrieve data from a particular provider, either for it to then handle it itself or to move it to another provider. Customer reluctance to move data into the cloud is partly explained by the fear of being locked into a particular vendor. The cloud industry recognizes this (primarily technical) challenge to make the cloud inter-operative so that it is easy for customers to exit one provider and migrate their data to another. There are a number of industry initiatives that fall under the broad umbrella term of 'open cloud' designed to facilitate such portability.

One such initiative is the Open Cloud Manifesto of March 2009 (heavily criticized by Microsoft at the time due to the secretive (non-open) nature of its development). This asks stakeholders who are involved in developing cloud services to bear in mind the following principles.

a) Cloud providers must be open and address in their offerings and through the adoption of standards the perceived challenges to cloud adoption (including security, portability and interoperability).

---

[71] See, for example, chapter 9.

b) Providers should avoid using their market position to lock customers into their proprietary platforms.

c) Providers should use and adopt existing standards wherever appropriate.

d) Providers should be pragmatic in relation to new standards and should avoid creating too many. Standards should promote innovation.

e) Open cloud efforts should be driven by customer needs, not proprietary technical interests.

f) Stakeholders should work together.

There are other similar efforts,[72] some developed in reaction to this Manifesto. They are all at too early a stage to merit full discussion in this book but the position will of course change. What might emerge through these processes (although we suspect it will take time) are industry standards which become widely accepted. If they do become accepted then of course customers may well explore adherence to these standards as part of diligence and seek to extract contractual assurances in relation to standards in this field as they do in relation to security.

14.3   Development of industry codes of practice

Out of the cloud industry are emerging a number of industry bodies (including, in Europe, EuroCloud and Cloud Industry Forum) generally promoting the industry and – as part of that promotion – trying to allay customer concerns. (The 'open cloud' initiatives just mentioned are one facet of this.)

For example, Cloud Industry Forum (CIF) (which includes Microsoft and RackSpace amongst its members) recognizes a number of issues which need to be addressed to reassure the public including:

– lack of transparency: the fact that professional-looking cloud services can be set up by small organizations without meaningful experience;[73]

– data protection, information security and service continuity;

– the anticipated dramatic speed of cloud take-over over the coming few years.

To that end, the CIF has prepared a 'code of practice' designed to allay those fears. Their aim is for such a code to become a recognized standard (supplemental to the more traditional information security standards such as ISO/IEC 27000 series) and so assist in bringing greater transparency and trust to the cloud. Suppliers could self-certify or obtain third-party certification accredited by the CIF.

---

[72]   For example, the Open Cloud Consortium, the Open Cloud Initiative or the Open Stack Initiative.

[73]   See 9.3.5

It is too early to say which (or if any) of these types of initiatives (there are others) will survive the passage of time in this fast moving industry.

14.4 Developments in data protection law

A number of developments might be expected over the short to medium term in data protection law. We have noted previously scepticism by German regulators[74] as to various aspects of data protection regulation compatibility with cloud computing. The UK ICO has not joined in with this scepticism and indeed seems to be adopting a more pragmatic and arguably business-friendly approach in the guidance it has issued so far.

Further, and more considered, guidance on the application of data protection rules to cloud computing will in due course no doubt come out from the Working Party and other regulators. Indeed, in its public work programme 2010–2011, the Working Party highlighted 'responding to technological challenges' (highlighting, within that, cloud computing) as one of the strategic themes it considers most relevant and urgent for consideration. Any pronouncement by the Working Party will be extremely important for cloud computing in Europe as it will inform both users as to their compliance responsibilities in this area and regulators as to their enforcement stance. It remains to be seen whether the Working Party as a whole (consisting of 27 national data protection regulators) will share the German regulators' scepticism.

Simultaneously with the Working Party continuing its work programme, the entire European data protection regime is under review. The UK ICO commissioned a review of the regime in 2008 and the resulting report was published in 2009.[75] In his foreword to the report, the then Information Commissioner, Richard Thomas, highlighted some of the strengths and weaknesses of the present Data Protection Directive [1] including the following weaknesses which resonate with the discussion on data protection in the cloud set out in this book.

- 'It the Directive is outdated, in terms of technology and regulatory approach.'

- 'Its scope is becoming increasingly unclear, for example in online and surveillance contexts.'

- 'Its international transfer rules are unrealistic against a backdrop of high-volume, globalised data flows.'

The UK regulator of course has no power to change the European rules; any such change would need a European level initiative. This is happening. Shortly after the UK initiative, the European Commission itself also initiated a review. A public

---

[74] See 5.4 and 6.3.3.
[75] Review of the European Data Protection Directive, Rand Europe, 2009 [44]. The quote is from the shorter 'summary report'.

consultation was held during the course of 2009 and a final recommendation for an updating of the Directive is expected by the end of 2011. Many of the responses to the consultation drew attention to the inability of the existing Directive to cope with modern technological developments including cloud (the Directive being largely negotiated before the modern prominence of the internet). It remains to be seen how, if at all, the European Union will respond to these developments. For those wanting the regime to be clarified so as to make it easier for customers to use the cloud without falling foul of data protection rules, there is no real grounds for optimism. One of the main drivers for the European level review is the technical (in a legal sense) issue of integrating data protection in the law enforcement arena properly into the general instrument. Another driver is to remove disparities in national implementations.

Finally on this topic, there is an interesting link with the 'open cloud' issue discussed in 14.2. One of the issues for discussion, set out in a paper prepared by the European Commission for stakeholder meetings held in mid 2010, was the following:

> 8. Is there a need to address the issue of 'data portability' in particular in the context of protection of personal data on the Internet, but also in the offline world? Should individuals always be able to permanently retrieve their own personal data from a certain application, and move it to another without being prevented by the data controller from doing so, either practically in terms of technical standards or contractually? [45]

14.5　Commoditization of cloud services

It is already possible for enterprise customers to buy infrastructure components (such as server instances) online with nothing more than a credit card. Provided that the 'open' cloud issues are dealt with, it is possible that customers will increasingly, perhaps, treat the acquisition of what would traditionally have been seen as a very static part of its operations (the data centre) as a very dynamic and agile thing. Server capacity (and service levels around them) may well then become standard resulting in there being only one differentiating factor: price. On contract renewal, there will be a desire to shop around only on the basis of that factor. In other words, cloud infrastructure may become commoditized, in the same way as certain types of goods (paper, coffee, and so on), oil and indeed electricity have become. If this were to happen, it may result in fewer (large) players, at least at the core infrastructure level, with many smaller entities fulfilling additional 'value added' services (system integration, support, and so on).

Might cloud (at least of the IaaS variety) really become 'commoditized' in this manner? It is too early to say, but there is an early indicator that it might. Amazon has introduced a dynamic pricing model so that users who are not reliant on capacity being available at particular times can pay as and when the price (depending on demand) drops to a particular 'spot' level. If the market continues to move in this direction so that trading follows, there may be some interesting legal consequences. Contracting may become simpler. Just as no-one (even enterprises) negotiates contracts with utility suppliers, so perhaps enterprises will – ignoring the lessons in this book – acquire capacity without much regard to the terms upon which the capacity is supplied. Then, as industries become commoditized, there can be trading in the base commodity. Amounts of the commodity can be bought and sold in bulk, and the supplier to the actual user may not in fact be someone who is primarily involved in the creation of the commodity. In the early part of this century, many thought that trading would occur in relation to bandwidth; but that never really happened to any meaningful level.[76] Might server and storage capacity be traded in this manner? We remain sceptical. Nonetheless, if there is this sort of commoditization then, just as with energy, coffee and metals, not only can the base product be traded (necessarily based on standard contracts), but the market will then ensure that 'derivative' products are built upon those exchanges; capacity might be 'hedged' (immunizing a user from too high a future price) and derivatives created with market participants trading even when they have absolutely no use for the underlying commodity.

This will be of little interest to users of cloud services (except to the extent they want to hedge their costs of acquiring those services). Most users will simply want to enjoy cloud services in as cost-effective, open, secure, regulatory compliant and contractually fair a manner as possible.

---

[76] An internet search of 'trading in bandwidth' for example will throw up many articles from the late 90s and early 00s, but none that are very recent. Enron was a big participant in this market before its demise.

Glossary

Amazon EC2	Amazon's Elastic Compute Cloud IaaS service which provides server capacity
Amazon S3	Amazon's Simple Storage Service IaaS service which provides storage
ASP (application service provision)	The provision of software applications remotely as a service; a predecessor term to SaaS
AUP (Acceptable Use Policy)	The rules set by a provider describing what a user can do with the service; designed primarily to shield the provider from liability to third parties or from itself being implicated (indirectly) in unlawful activity.
Data controller	The company, body or other person that determines the purposes and means of the processing of personal data; responsible for data protection compliance
Data processor	The company, body or other that processes personal data on behalf of the controller; does not have its own data protection compliance responsibilities under data protection law
Data protection principles	Eight principles set out in the DPA, with which a data controller must comply
Directive (Data Protection Directive)	Directive 95/46/EC of the European Parliament and of the Council of 24 October 1995 on the protection of individuals with regard to the processing of personal data and on the free movement of such data
DPA	Data Protection Act 1998; the implementation of the Directive in the UK
EEA (European Economic Area)	The European Union together with Iceland, Liechtenstein and Norway

Eighth (data protection) principle	The data protection principle that requires the data controller not to transfer personal data outside the EEA unless 'adequate' safeguards are in place
Google App Engine	A PaaS service offered by Google
IaaS (infrastructure as a service)	The provision of computing infrastructure (such as server or storage capacity) through a remotely provided service
ICO	Information Commissioner's Office; the UK data protection regulator
Instance	in the context of software as a service, an occurrence of the software running on a server. A provider may have many instances running on different servers (or on the same server)
ISMS	Information Security Management System
ISO/IEC 27000 series	A series of information security management standards (ISMS) published jointly by the International Organization for Standardization (ISO) and the International Electrotechnical Commission (IEC)
Multi-tenancy	A term that describes the fact that one particular instance of software is simultaneously handling the data of a number of cloud customers (the 'tenants') on the provider's server
PaaS (platform as a service)	The provision of a platform allowing the development and then deployment of new software applications. A prominent example is Google App Engine
Personal data	Data about identifiable individuals; the subject of data protection legislation
SaaS (software as a service)	The delivery of a software application remotely by the provider over the internet; perhaps through a web interface
Safe Harbor scheme	A scheme under which US entities can self-certify to an overarching set of data protection principles and so facilitate the transfer to them of personal data from Europe
SAS 70	The Statement on Auditing Standards No. 70 (SAS 70), and auditing standard developed by the American Institute of Certified Public Accountants (AICPA)

Seventh (data protection) principle	The data protection principle that requires the data controller to ensure personal data is kept secure
Standard clauses	One of the three different types of model contracts approved by the European Commission to ensure compliance with the eighth principle.
US Patriot Act	US legislation that gives wide powers to law enforcement agencies to obtain intelligence for criminal investigatory and anti-terrorist purposes
Virtualization	Technology that enables an enterprise to operate software on a 'virtual' server (which could be spread across a number of different physical servers) rather than on a specific physical server
Windows Azure	A PaaS service offered by Microsoft
Working Party or Article 29 Working Party	The body set up by Article 29 of the Directive to provide guidance on the operation of the Directive. There are 27 members of the Working Party; one from each of the EU member states

Bibliography

[1] EUROPEAN COMMUNITIES. 95/46/EC. Directive of the European
     Parliament and of the Council of 24 October 1995 on the protection of
     individuals with regard to the processing of personal data and on the free
     movement of such data (Data Protection Directive). Luxembourg: Office for
     Official Publications of the European Communities, 1995.

[2] Council Regulation (EC) No. 593/2008 of the European Parliament and of
     the Council of 17 June 2008 on the law applicable to contractual obligations
     (Rome I), OJ 2008 No. L177/6, 04 July 2008.

[3] Council Regulation (EC) No 864/2007 of the European Parliament and
     of the Council of 11 July 2007 on the law applicable to non-contractual
     obligations (Rome II), OJ 2007 No. L199/40, 31 July 2007.

[4] GREAT BRITAIN. The Unfair Contract Terms Act 1977. London: The
     Stationery Office.

[5] EUROPEAN COMMUNITIES. 2000/31/EC. Directive of the European
     Parliament and of the Council of 8 June 2000 on certain legal aspects of
     information society services, in particular electronic commerce, in the Internal
     Market (Directive on electronic commerce). Luxembourg: Office for Official
     Publications of the European Communities, 2000.

[6] UNITED STATES OF AMERICA. US Patriot Act 2001. Washington:
     Government Printing Office.

[7] GREAT BRITAIN. The Regulation of Investigatory Powers Act 2000.
     London: The Stationery Office.

[8] GREAT BRITAIN. Intelligence Services Act 1994. London: The Stationery
     Office.

[9] GREAT BRITAIN. Police Act 1997. London: The Stationery Office.

[10] CANADA. The Freedom of Information and Protection of Privacy Act 1993.
     Washington: Government Printing Office.

[11] ISO Publication – ISO/IEC 27001, *Information technology — Security techniques — Information security management systems — Requirements.*

[12] ISO Publication – ISO/IEC 27002, *Information technology – Security techniques – Code of practice for information security management.*

[13] American Institute of CPAs, S*tatement on Auditing Standards No. 70: Service Organizations (SAS 70)*, New York: AICPA, May 2009.

[14] BSI Publication – BS 7799 series, *Information security management.*

[15] BSI Publication – BS 17799 series, *Information technology.*

[16] GREAT BRITAIN. Data Protection Act 1998. London: The Stationery Office.

[17] ISO Publication – ISO/IEC 27011, *Information technology — Security techniques — Information security management guidelines for telecommunications organizations based on ISO/IEC 27002.*

[18] EUROPEAN COMMUNITIES. Opinion 10/2006 of 22 November 2006 on the processing of personal data by the Society for Worldwide Interbank Financial Telecommunication (SWIFT) (WP 128).

[19] EUROPEAN COMMUNITIES. Opinion 1/2010 of 16 February 2010 on the concepts of 'controller' and 'processor' (WP 169).

[20] Information Commissioner's Office (ICO) Publication – *The Guide to Data Protection*, London: ICO, 2009.

[21] Information Commissioner's Office (ICO) Publication – *Outsourcing – a guide for small and medium-sized businesses*, London: ICO, 2009.

[22] Information Commissioner's Office (ICO) Publication – *Personal information online Code of Practice*, London: ICO, July 2010.

[23] UNITED STATES OF AMERICA. Health Insurance Portability and Accountability Act (HIPAA). Washington: Government Printing Office.

[24] UNITED STATES OF AMERICA. The Gramm-Leach-Bliley Act 1999 (also known as the Financial Services Modernization Act of 1999). Washington: Government Printing Office.

[25] UNITED STATES OF AMERICA. Children's Online Privacy Protection Act of 1998 (COPPA). Washington: Government Printing Office.

[26] EUROPEAN COMMUNITIES. 2002/58/EC. Directive of the European Parliament and of the Council of 12 July 2002 concerning the processing of personal data and the protection of privacy in the electronic communications

sector. Luxembourg: Office for Official Publications of the European Communities, 2002.

[27] EUROPEAN COMMUNITIES. 2009/136/EC. Directive of the European Parliament and of the Council of 25 November 2009 on the regulatory framework for electronic communications networks and services (e-privacy Directive), amending Directive 2002/22/EC on universal service and users' rights relating to electronic communications networks and services, Directive 2002/58/EC concerning the processing of personal data and the protection of privacy in the electronic communications sector and Regulation (EC) No 2006/2004 on cooperation between national authorities responsible for the enforcement of consumer protection laws. Luxembourg: Office for Official Publications of the European Communities, 2009.

[28] Financial Services Authority. *Financial Services Authority (FSA) Handbook*. London: FSA, 2005.

[29] Financial Services Authority. *Data Security in Financial Services*. London: FSA, April 2008.

[30] GREAT BRITAIN. Unfair Terms in Consumer Contracts Regulations 1999. London: The Stationery Office.

[31] GREAT BRITAIN. Financial Services and Markets Act (FSMA) 2000. London: The Stationery Office.

[32] EUROPEAN COMMUNITIES. 2004/39/EC. Directive of the European Parliament and of the Council of 21 April 2004 on markets in financial instruments (MiFID) amending Council Directives 85/611/EEC and 93/6/EEC and Directive 2000/12/EC of the European Parliament and of the Council and repealing Council Directive 93/22/EEC. Luxembourg: Office for Official Publications of the European Communities, 2004.

[33] EUROPEAN COMMUNITIES. Capital Requirements Directive (CRD), comprising of 2006/48/EC of the European Parliament and of the Council of 14 June 2006 relating to the taking up and pursuit of the business of credit institutions, and 2006/49/EC of the European Parliament and of the Council of 14 June 2006 on the capital adequacy of investment firms and credit institutions. Luxembourg: Office for Official Publications of the European Communities, 2006.

[34] GREAT BRITAIN. Public Contracts Regulations 2006. London: The Stationery Office.

[35] GREAT BRITAIN. Freedom of Information Act (FOIA) 2000. London: The Stationery Office.

[36] GREAT BRITAIN. The Electronic Commerce (EC Directive) Regulations 2002. London: The Stationery Office.

[37] UNITED STATES OF AMERICA. Digital Millennium Copyright Act 1998. Washington: Government Printing Office.

[38] GREAT BRITAIN. Defamation Act 1996. London: The Stationery Office.

[39] GREAT BRITAIN. Obscene Publications Act 1959. London: The Stationery Office.

[40] GREAT BRITAIN. Protection of Children Act 1978. London: The Stationery Office.

[41] GREAT BRITAIN. Criminal Justice Act 1988. London: The Stationery Office.

[42] GREAT BRITAIN. Electronic Commerce Directive (Terrorism Act 2006) Regulations 2007. London: The Stationery Office.

[43] EUROPEAN COMMUNITIES. Opinion 5/2009 of 12 June 2009 on online social networking (WP 163).

[44] Information Commissioner's Office (ICO) Publication – *Review of the European Data Protection Directive*, London: Rand Europe, 2009

[45] Stakeholders' Consultations, 'Future of data protection', Background paper: http://ec.europa.eu/justice_home/news/events/data_protection_regulatory_framework/background_paper_en.pdf

Index

NOTE   Footnotes have also been referenced within this index in cases where additional information may be useful to the reader. These entries refer to the page on which the footnote appears and the number of the note, for example '53n22' refers to page 53, note 22.

If you found this book useful, you may also want to buy:

Managing Security in Outsourced and Off-shored Environments: How to safeguard intellectual assets in a virtual business world
David Lacey

The book sets out guidance, learning points, best practices and critical success factors associated with managing the security risks associated with outsourcing and off-shoring of IT and business services. The content is presented in an accessible language and structured in a logical sequence reflecting the life-cycle of outsourcing, from inception through definition, selection, negotiation, implementation and ongoing management of outsourced services.

Building on both practical, real-life experience of implementing and managing large scale outsourcing programmes, as well as recent research sponsored by the UK Government Cyber Security Knowledge Transfer Network, the author sets out a set of practical guidelines in plain business language that addresses the wide range of risks associated with outsourcing and off-shoring contracts. In particular, the book focuses on the critical "softer" management issues, such as strategy, risk assessment and relationship management, which ultimately determine the success of a major outsourcing programme.

- **A5 paperback • ISBN 978 0 580 68701 3 • 187pp • £24.95 • May 2010**
- **For more details see http://shop.bsigroup.com/bip0116**

Information Security Risk Management: Handbook for ISO/IEC 27001 – *Edward Humphreys*

The focus of this book is based around the concept of having an information security management system (ISMS) as a framework for achieving the effective management of information security risks. International standard ISO/IEC 27001 is a world recognized standard for establishing, implementing, monitoring and reviewing, updating and improving an ISMS. ISO/IEC 27005 is an ISMS risk management standard that supports the implementation of ISO/IEC 27001.

This book is aimed at those business managers and staff involved in ISMS risk management activities. It is a practical handbook for the use and application of ISO/IEC 27005. It provides guidance and advice to specifically support the implementation of those requirements specified in ISO/IEC 27001:2005 that relate to risk management processes and associated activities.

- **A5 paperback • ISBN 9780 580 60745 5 • 156pp • £38.95 • April 2010**
- **For more details see http://shop.bsigroup.com/bip0076**